# Music From Another World

Simon Laks and René Coudy

Translated from the French by
Virginie Actis and John Knych
With essays by André Laks,
Annette Becker, and Frank Harders-Wuthenow

*Pristim Editions*

First published in 2024 by Printim Editions

Printed and bound by TJ Books 2024

ISBN 979-8-9874792-8-5

Copyright © Printim Editions 2024

The right of André Laks to be identified as the owner of this work has been asserted by him in accordance with the Copyright, Designs and Patents Act 1988.

All rights reserved. No part of this publication may be reproduced, stored in a retrieval system, or transmitted, in any form, or by any means (electronic, mechanical, photocopying, recording or otherwise) without the permission of the publisher.

Translated from French into English by Virginie Actis and John Knych

First Edition

Originally published as *Musique d'un autre monde* (1948) by Mercure de France, Paris

228 Park Avenue S.
New York, NY 10003
www.printimeditions.com

# CONTENTS

Editorial Note . . . . . . . . . . . . . . . . . . . . . . . .7

**Simon Laks and René Coudy, *Music From Another World***
Preface by Georges Duhamel. . . . . . . . . . . . . . . . . 11

|      |                        |     |
|------|------------------------|-----|
|      | Overture               | 13  |
| i.   | Alla tedesca           | 17  |
| ii.  | Invitation to the Muse | 22  |
| iii. | First Sounds           | 25  |
| iv.  | Quatuor                | 31  |
| v.   | Aubade                 | 37  |
| vi.  | Broken Cadences        | 41  |
| vii. | Duo                    | 45  |
| viii.| Soli                   | 49  |
| ix.  | Fragile Consonances    | 53  |
| x.   | Music First!           | 60  |
| xi.  | Modulations            | 64  |
| xii. | Theme and Variations   | 71  |
| xiii.| Suite                  | 77  |
| xiv. | Presto con fuoco       | 84  |
| xv.  | Symphony of Chaos      | 89  |
| xvi. | Serenades              | 94  |
| xvii.| Directed Cacophony     | 99  |
| xviii.| Romances              | 106 |
| xix. | SS and Sainte-Cécile   | 115 |
| xx.  | Decrescendo            | 124 |
| xxi. | Seventh of the Dominant| 130 |
| xxii.| Final Chord            | 135 |

André Laks, "About My Father" . . . . . . . . . . . . .139
Annette Becker, "Simon Laks, *Music From Another World*
              A Jewish composer in Auschwitz-Birkenau". . . .151
Frank Harders-Wuthenow, "The Composer Simon Laks" . . . . .189
Glossary . . . . . . . . . . . . . . . . . . . . . . . . .205
First Readers . . . . . . . . . . . . . . . . . . . . . .209

# Editorial Note

Shortly after his return to France from the Auschwitz-Birkenau extermination camp, Simon Laks (Warsaw 1901–Paris 1983), a composer by trade, wrote in collaboration with René Coudy, a fellow deportee, a book entitled *Musique d'un autre monde* (*Music of Another World*).[1] This book was published by Mercure de France in 1948 with a preface by Georges Duhamel and awarded a Prix spécial *Vérité*. In this memoir, Laks recounted how the camp orchestra he conducted for over two years had saved him and his friend from certain death. Thirty years later, Simon Laks, who had lost track of René Coudy, reworked and updated the book in Polish, which he published with *Oficyna Poetów i Malarzy* (*Poets' and Painters' Press*) under the title *Gry Oświęcimski* (1979, reissued by Auschwitz Museum Editions)—an apt title in Polish but difficult to translate literally into another language (it would be: *Auschwitzian Plays*, like 'playing' music and like 'play' as in 'play a game'). It was this second book that was published in English by Northwestern University Press in 1989, under a title, *Music of Another World*, that only shared the title of the 1948 book, but not the content, which is obviously a source of confusion. The French translation of the reworked Polish book is *Mélodies d'Auschwitz* (i.e. *Auschwitzian Melodies*), first published by Editions du Cerf in 1991.[2]

The present volume contains the translation of the 1948 French book with a slight variation of its original title, *Music From Another World*. One important difference with the 1979 book is that the "I" who speaks in *Music From Another World* is René Coudy, while Simon Laks, "the real complete musician" (p. 32), is called André, the name he was to give to his son two years after the writing of the book.

The book is enriched by three essays devoted to the life and work of Simon Laks, who had begun a career as a composer in Paris before the Second World War, which he continued as best he could after the war. The essays are the work of historian Annette Becker, musicologist Frank Harders-Wuthenow, and Simon's son André Laks. The set thus offers an indispensable complement to the Northwestern University Press publication, where the translation of the 1979 Polish book is not illuminated by any information or perspective.[3]

Terms left in German in the book and essays are not always translated in the originals. They are explained in the Glossary.

This volume would not have been possible without the initiative and hard work of Virginie Actis and John Knych, to whom we offer our warmest thanks for their commitment.

Annette Becker and André Laks

---

1. The cover of the original book is reproduced on page 9.

2. The two books, written thirty years apart, appear side by side in the expanded French edition published by Editions du Cerf in 2018 under the title *Mélodies d'Auschwitz et autres écrits sur les camps*, which contains, in addition to a former version of the three essays translated here, a number of accompanying documents, alluded to by Annette Becker in her afterword. To avoid confusions, the references to the 1979 book published by Northwestern University Press will use the abbreviation *AM* (for *Auschwitzian Melodies*).

3. See also the Preface that the historian Pierre Vidal-Naquet has written for the first edition (Cerf, 1991) of *Mélodies d'Auschwitz* ("Les harmoniques de Simon Laks"). It is reprinted in his *Réflexions sur le génocide. Les Juifs, la mémoire et le présent*, tome 3 (La Découverte,1995, p. 185-193).

SIMON LAKS ET RENÉ COUDY

# MUSIQUES
## D'UN
# AUTRE MONDE

*Préface de Georges Duhamel
de l'Académie Française*

PARIS
MERCVRE DE FRANCE
XXVI, RVE DE CONDÉ, XXVI
MCMXLVIII

# Preface

by Georges Duhamel,
member of the *Académie Française*

We, men of the West, thought we had a thousand chances, each more awful than the next, to measure the abyss of degradation into which humanity plunged itself through the mad and the sick to whom, for twenty years, the Germanic world surrendered its destiny.

We, men of France, having read book after book, testimonies of countless narrators whose good faith no one can doubt, since they all say the same thing, we thought we had, with them, visited all the circles of hell.

This crisis of cruel insanity, this crisis that has perverted almost an entire people and for a long time filled civilized societies with suffering and shame, it seemed to us, anguished observers, that it was now subject to the judgment of historians, that investigation was closed and that, on the confused drama that tortured so many victims and revealed so many executioners, we knew everything that could be known.

It seems that we were wrong.

To all those who would intend to maintain some illusion on this point, I advise them to read chapter XIX of the book composed by Mr. Simon Laks and Mr. René Coudy. I advise them, in particular, to turn their attention to the end of this chapter and to the confidences of SS Wolff. They will see that Mephistopheles is not the figment of a poet's imagination, but the figure, constantly revived, of a truly national hero.

With resigned desolation we would bear with this sordidness if, at least, our last refuges were spared in this universal shipwreck, if, at least, we had the feeling that in spite of everything the immaterial goods for us would still have a consoling and redeeming value and be preserved from all defilement.

The book brought to us by two Auschwitz survivors seems likely to take away any element of comfort. It teaches us that the executioners in the German camps were sensitive to music. Yes, holy music, divine music is also compromised in the adventure!

Every man, after reading this book, can retire for an hour in solitude. He can, with the help of faith or reason, compose a prayer. He is no longer even sure of this supreme asylum: he may learn one day that the torturers also prayed, in their own way, in their own language and according to the impulses of their desperate genius.

—*Georges Duhamel,* member of the *Académie Française*

# OVERTURE

Towards the end of 1943, the prisoners of Auschwitz II-Birkenau were authorized by the German camp command to send a written message to their families.

To be exact, I[1] should not use the word "authorized" because in fact it was an order whose execution was going to be scrupulously controlled. Also, those who did not want to submit addressed their letters to imaginary people. These postcards could have revealed, if they were sincere, the places where many of the elements sought by the Gestapo were to be found or hidden. More than one prisoner had been suspicious of them. Most of our comrades saw them as propaganda.

However, certain conditions were imposed on us: a limited number of words, a ban on soliciting money or parcels, to speak only of oneself, and to indicate this original address: *Arbeitslager* Birkenau being Neu-Berun, i.e., Birkenau Work Camp, when in reality our address should have been: *Konzentrations- und Vernichtungslager* [Concentration and Extermination Camp] Birkenau-Auschwitz II.

Driven by the desire to let my loved ones know that I was alive and convinced that this was the only chance to do so, I wrote to my loved ones that "I was healthy and working in my profession." My profession being that of musician, I thought I was making them understand that I had an easy job.

When I saw my wife again after my release, she informed me that she had received this card. She had never believed, however, that I was really working in my profession, and assumed that I had written this to put her mind at rest.

Who, indeed, could have believed that such a job existed in a German camp?

---

1. As explained in the Editorial Note (above, p. 7), "I" is René Coudy. Simon Laks will be designated as André later in the text (p. 32).

Two years have passed since the liberation and despite all the investigations that have been made, despite the quantity of books that have been published, despite even the films made about the concentration camps, my interlocutors are always amazed every time I talk to them about Auschwitz in general and its musical activity in particular.

How, they say, was there music in your camp? What was it used for? What was its purpose? What did you play? Funeral marches?

I was asked many other questions. All of them seemed naive, but justified, given the complete ignorance of the question.

There was actually a musical ensemble—Commando *Lagerkapelle*—in Auschwitz, just as there was one in every German camp that "respected itself." And this music, an essential part of the organization of the camps, was, as paradoxical as it may seem, an accessory, and not the least, of its internal police force.

The very first ambition of a *Lagerführer* (camp commander) was to constitute "his" *Lagerkapelle*, to ensure the impeccable functioning of the disciplinary machine and also, as we shall see in these pages, for the personal entertainment and maintenance of the morale of the SS herd, our guards.

It is not the purpose of this book to describe, once again, the horrors and atrocities of which Auschwitz was the theater. If from time to time we cannot avoid evoking them it is to make the text more understandable.

Much has been written about the Nazi camps and we do not think it is necessary to add new, even unpublished, documents. Everything happened there in a universe of infinity. Whether we multiply this infinity by ten, a hundred, or a thousand, we always remain in this infinity. Beyond a certain limit, human suffering ceases to be perceptible and definable for those who have not gone beyond it. We who "saw it" did not want to believe, neither at the beginning nor later, that it was possible. How, then, could the authenticity of the facts be accepted by those who had not witnessed them?

Auschwitz was in a way a kind of 'negative' of the world we had left. Our most essential dignities were regarded as vices, our sense of logic was interpreted as a symptom of insanity, while our most vile instincts, repressed by the education we had received, had become undeniable virtues and one of the conditions for our survival. Thus, the aristocracy of the camp generally included bandits, common criminals, professional assassins, while intellectuals, artists, scholars, and priests formed the underbelly of this new society, invented by the German genius.

Only a very small number of deportees returned. Does this prove the humanity of whoever reacted predictably to this change in environment, from the first contact with a world whose existence they were far from suspecting? How many perished after a few days, often a few hours after their arrival! All those who survived Auschwitz do not owe it exclusively to the factors of luck, endurance, will, or resistance. Indeed, these factors contributed greatly to our salvation, but they would certainly have been insufficient if we had not understood, with lightning speed, that in order not to succumb immediately, we had to rid ourselves of a major part of our old morals, of our "humanity," of all the prejudices of our civilization, in short, to assimilate ourselves by all means to the society of which we were henceforth to be a part, to its way of thinking, its morals, its feelings, its educational spirit, and its laws.

We are well aware that from having lived both instinctively and consciously in this climate of adoption, we have all become more or less inhuman and often shocking to the society that has fortunately reintegrated us. A deep abyss separates us from it, perhaps forever.

Its literary, moral, sentimental, and even humorous vocabulary is far too poor to plead in our favor. The most faithful accounts, the most meticulous descriptions will never reflect reality as we have experienced it. We do not pretend to fill this abyss, knowing that it is something impossible to achieve. We are a bit like Pirandellian characters in search of an author capable of telling our adventure. But we are sure we will never find one.

That is why, although we are not writers and although we realize that the task we have undertaken is beyond our means, we want to talk. Our pretensions are modest. We wish to make known an unknown and authentic page in the history of Auschwitz II-Birkenau.

As part of the *Lagerkapelle*, we have had the sad privilege of observing almost all the workings of the camp, not only the "atrocities" but also the conception, organization, method, and results expected for the immediate and distant future. It is around us, musicians, that the heterogeneous world that populated Auschwitz revolved, be it the SS or the inmates. And we believe that we, more than anyone else, had the opportunity, on the one hand, to get to know the German soul, and on the other hand, to closely follow the psychological vicissitudes of the Auschwitz inmates, our brothers in misery.

# I. ALLA TEDESCA

When we got off the cattle train that had taken us across Germany to Auschwitz, we were sorted: on one side the old men (the women and children were loaded onto trucks parked on the platform) and on the other side the younger men, including myself, were lined up in columns of a hundred, each consisting of twenty rows of five people.

This is thus how I saw myself, without expecting it in the least, separated from my parents.

After undergoing a cursory check of our numbers by the Germans, we set off, flanked by a dozen armed soldiers. My neighbor, knowing a little bit of German, tried to have a conversation with the soldier who was marching beside us. He was quite talkative. In the midst of justified anxiety, I interrupted this conversation from time to time to ask my companion to translate for me what the German was saying. He did so not without reluctance, as if he wanted to keep these revelations to himself. However, I came to know them little by little.

The trucks would transport the old and the weak to a special camp, reserved for easy work. As for us, young and of strong constitution, we were going to be assigned to various jobs, according to the aptitudes of each one. Our luggage, left on the arrival platform, would be returned to us inside the camp as soon as the control and hygiene formalities were completed. We would be able to see our families every Sunday, provided that we behaved well.

I felt the tension in my chest loosen. I was not afraid of work, even very hard work. And I thought that I would work all the more courageously because I would receive the promised reward at the end of the week.

After half an hour's walk, our column stopped in front of a red building that looked very gloomy. We had undoubtedly just arrived at the camp which was intended for us.

I am trying to clearly reconstruct my first memories of Auschwitz. I am struggling to do so. I have the feeling that I experienced these things at the time of my early childhood. Only furtive images remain. They are vague impressions rather than memories.

I hear foul swearing and guttural utterances from strange, rowdy characters, robust like professional wrestlers, wearing red or yellow armbands and equipped with sturdy clubs that fall on our faces and backs constantly and for any reason. They are not German soldiers, these individuals are prisoners, like us, dressed in striped convict costumes or civilian suits with clearly visible red lines painted on the back of the jacket and on the pants. While taking off our caps in front of our SS guards, as each one of us must do, they talk to them almost as equals, confide in them with a familiarity that seems inappropriate to me and seem to enjoy our misery with all their heart. They are the ones who direct us from one service to another, they are the ones who distribute our food to us, and finally they are the ones who represent for us the supreme authority.

I see myself naked, in endless queues, sometimes in barracks, sometimes outside in the mud, under an icy shower, to undergo the relentless protocol of camp hygiene: a haircut and a shower as cold as the rain, followed by a frantic run through the mud with a new accompaniment of rain and blows with sticks. Then we are waiting in front of piles of packets in a building with a cement floor and no windows, waiting to be handed a packet of rags to be used as our clothing. We are still waiting for a number to be assigned to us, which from now on will replace our social identity. I no longer have a first or last name, and my only identification is this number tattooed on my left forearm. We are constantly waiting... without knowing exactly what we are waiting for. Today is Wednesday and there are still three long days left until Sunday!

If this wait could only come to an end! Whether they take us to work or let us sleep... or at least sit down! The cold penetrates us, the hunger pulls at us, we are harassed, exhausted, at the end of strength and patience.

Finally, all kinds of containers are distributed to us. There are pots, empty cans, spittoons, chamber pots, there are also real camp bowls, in the shape of salad bowls with a capacity of about two liters. A barrel is brought on a kind of stretcher, by two athletes who put it on the ground. A shout is heard:

"Put yourself in groups of five! *Zu fünfe!*"

And it is again a fight, blows raining down upon on us, men collapse, others rush to the barrel to draw the grayish liquid it contains. The blows increase in frequency and violence.

The men are finally arranged in groups of five. One of the red-armed, rowdy characters uses a large ladle to reluctantly pour a tiny part of the liquid into the bowl of those who, calmed by the blows, now advance obediently, still in fives. From time to time, the soup attendant will strike a blow with his sticky ladle to those who have the misfortune to anticipate or delay the prescribed order. As soon as they are served, the men must be pulled over to the other side of the barracks to prevent them going to the distribution a second time. And it is always by five, infallibly by five, that they line up.

Five! This is the fateful number of the German camp. "*Zu Fünfe!*" by five—and "*Aufgehen zu fünfe!*"—Complete with five! are the eternal refrains. Knowing how to line up by five, how to fill a hole in the previous row, it doesn't sound like anything, yet it's quite an art for a prisoner! I learned it in the end and relatively quickly, but at what a price! How many have had to pay with their lives for their inability to adapt, while walking or even at rest, to this invariable discipline!

After three days and three nights of interminable "formalities" I find myself, at the end of my physical and moral strength, huddled against a wall of the barracks. I can finally extend my bruised limbs. Lying, like my companions in misfortune, on the floor paved with poorly joined bricks, I feel my eyelids closing, but it is impossible for me to sleep. The image of my parents haunts me constantly. I already know that I won't see them, not tomorrow on Sunday, nor ever again. The hairdresser who cut my hair—a Parisian like me and who has been at the camp for a long time already—has informed me of the plight of my father and mother, as well as of the fate that is reserved for me. I am no longer unaware that my parents were murdered and that I myself will not get out of here alive. There is just enough time to offer the little physical strength I have left as an offering to the Nazi Moloch to compensate him for the costs of my maintenance: four or five weeks at the most.

A torpor invades my limbs and I slowly fall asleep. An excruciating hunger gnaws at me. Where are you, gingerbread and sweets left in my luggage? Why didn't I eat you before the end of the trip! My poor parents... For a moment, I lose all notion of reality and I am transported in thought to the life of the past. Home, work, my friends, my juvenile loves... How far away it all seems to me, immaterial!

Suddenly, I jump in a burst of unspeakable joy. I am convinced that I am having an abominable nightmare, and that all I have to do is wake up and chase it away forever! I get up, rub my eyes, and look around me.

Alas! No. The reality is there, cruel, inexorable. A weak light bulb lights up the gloomy decor of my barracks. A long row of inert bodies, wrapped in rags, piled up against each other, moving from time to time to scratch or change position. These were, some time ago, normal human beings, human beings who lived, worked, hoped... Yes, the reality is there! I can refuse to accept it, but I will have to submit to it.

I go back to bed and plunge again into torpor. I see myself caught in a horrible mousetrap, with no way out. Outside, there is war, things are happening, people are fighting for a cause. And here I am, lying on an odious pallet, like the last of the vagabonds. Wouldn't it be better to get it over with? But how could it be done?

A shotgun blast outside, then a second one. I shudder with anguish. What is the meaning of this? Who is being shot?

Silence. Sleep finally wins me over and, this time, for good.

# II. INVITATION TO THE MUSE

I am awakened from my sleep by a dreadful racket. I feel like I've hardly slept for two hours. I jump up with the others. Sticks are waving around the sleepers, sometimes falling flat, sometimes pricking the most sensitive parts of their bodies with their tips. Strident cries resound from all sides: "*Aufstehen*!"—Get up! "*Raus*"—Out! We don't have to get dressed or put on shoes, not having undressed and not having shoes. We get up in a hurry, our heads jolt against one another, our bodies bump into each other, we find it difficult to regain our balance. We dash outside, avoiding as best we can the bullies armed with clubs who chase us.

It is still dark. It's barely raining, but it's still cold. Here we are gathered in a place, between two barracks: "*Los!*"—Quickly! "*Zu fünfe!*"—someone's yelling and screaming. Once again, there is a disorderly rush to get into the required order. It takes a long time before we have settled down satisfactorily. But here, a new torment awaits us.

There is a second art, which no prisoner can ignore or risk losing his life, that of collective salute on command. The perfection in the execution of this rite is judged by the magnitude of the slap, rigorously simultaneous, produced by our caps which, held in the hand, fall violently on the right thigh. The operation is carried out in four stages, the first two of which are devoted to the removal of the headgear and the last two to its replacement. At one command, the right hand is brought to the beret and at the next—and this is where the great art lies—the beret is brutally removed by dropping it on the thigh with the maximum possible noise. The second phase is the reverse of the previous one, and the clacking is caused, this time, by the palm of the empty hand falling back on the leg, which is much less difficult, because it is less rigorously controlled.

## II. INVITATION TO THE MUSE

This exercise is imposed on us for more than an hour. It is extremely tiring, not only for us who perform it, but also for those who instruct us. To let their throat, arms, elbows, and feet rest, which take an active part in this initiation, our tutors take turns several times.

In the meantime, the day has dawned, black and grim. The fog prevents any prognosis. Will the sun finally deign to show itself? We haven't seen it since we arrived.

Our torturers seem somewhat satisfied with their students and after several recommendations that sound like threats, they are put to rest. Taking advantage of the fact that nobody is watching us for the moment, we sit on the ground. From my seat, I can see what is going on around us.

It's getting lighter and lighter. A back-and forth-movement begins to appear in every corner of the camp and intensifies from minute to minute. Steaming barrels, presumably containing a beverage, are carried by small groups of men along what appears to be the central walkway. Sickly teenagers, early convicts, run in different directions, carrying written or shouted messages. In front of one of the barracks at the end of the camp I can make out a group of men sitting or lying on the ground, looking miserable, some dressed in rags, while others are naked or wearing soiled shirts. I am told that they are sick people waiting to be hospitalized. I am distracted from this spectacle by an incident. One of the barrels, supported by makeshift means, has slipped between the hands of the porters and collapsed while pouring the boiling liquid on the ground. The men are shouting in pain. I don't know if it's because of their burns or because of the blows they receive from the red armbands that are running up and down from all sides. I turn my eyes away, wondering what the next grueling vision will be.

I then see, in the alley, a few men loaded with wooden objects whose shape seems to be familiar. The idea seems so absurd to me that I find it hard to admit that these objects are indeed those I believe.

As the men approach, I open my eyes wider. Could it be a mirage? Nevertheless, I have to face the facts. I can now clearly distinguish the shape of these objects. No doubt about it, they are music stands, music stands! The men go towards the entrance of the camp and put them in a place that seems to have been created for this purpose.

My observations are interrupted by a hoarse cry. I mechanically monkey the others. Following the rhythm of the screams, I stand at attention and perform the ritual gestures of salute on command, in front of the SS who proceed to the morning roll call.

I am in the greatest of confusions. In this atmosphere of misfortune, these stands that I have just seen are the symbol of music, one of the images of freedom and independence of spirit. My thoughts weave chaotically throughout my brain, like the evocative superimpositions of dreams. They overlap, going from despair to doubt, from uncertainty to hope. I cling greedily, by a vestige of logic, to the idea engendered by this recent vision. Let us reason. Where there are music stands there are musicians, the former without the latter has no reason to exist. So who plays music here? The executioners or the victims? What is the music that resounds in this cursed place? Macabre dances? Funeral marches? Hitlerian songs? Thus, I ask myself a long series of questions, similar to those my friends will ask me when I return to France after my liberation. As a dazzling answer to these questions, I suddenly hear bawling, in French:

"Are there any musicians among you?"

## III. FIRST SOUNDS

I rush out of line and run to the person who has just made that call. He is a middle-aged man, strongly built, dressed in the striped suit I have already mentioned; his shaved white hair gives him an air of authority that imposes itself on me and holds me in respect before him. He looks at me with a kind of contempt and asks me in French what my specialty is. He seems to be consulting another character who stands beside him and to whom he translates my answers into German. This one has a completely different figure, although he also gives off a martial look. He is a rather tall man, almost sickly thin. He wears a civilian suit which, contrary to our rags, is of a sought-after cut, as if it had been made to measure by the best tailor in London. A short overcoat is casually thrown over his shoulders and one of his sleeves is adorned with a black silk armband, on which is finely embroidered a silver lyre, the emblem of music.

I feel very small in front of these two men, whose cleanliness and elegance clash with what I see around me. After answering the white-haired man's questions and showing him the number tattooed on my arm, I am dismissed from the ranks with the recommendation to report to barracks 15 at nine o'clock.

I use the time I have left to sit in a corner of my barracks, while trying to order the impressions I have just gathered. From afar, vague echoes of music reach my ears, without me being able to distinguish the character. However, I perceive very clearly bass drum strokes, beaten in a monotonous and barbaric rhythm, by alternating two and three strokes. One might think that it is the beat of an infernal machine animated by a perpetual movement, to push the nerves to the limit. I hear these bass drum strokes for about an hour, then they suddenly stop in complete silence. I have no notion of what time it might be. The manager of the barracks provides me with this piece of information as he hands out my bread ration. I then walk around the camp, while nibbling my bread. This recklessness earns me a few blows from several striped individuals, whom I was apparently wrong not to distrust and who ask me the reason for my idleness. But each time the word "music" brings about a magical change in their attitude. They amicably pat me on the shoulder and leave me in peace.

The camp is almost empty. The few people I meet seem to be in the internal service, while most of the inmates are probably working outside the camp. Those who remain come and go from different sides, sometimes walking peacefully, sometimes running at full speed. From time to time a shout is heard from a small building on the other side of the barbed wire, near the entrance. This cry is immediately taken up by those who heard it first and repeated successively from one end of the camp to the other. This is how the SS guards summon the civil servant prisoners. The cry resounds until the person sought is found and has presented himself, at full speed, before the SS who requested him.

I see, rushing out of a shack, the hairdresser who had confided in me. He was just called by the Germans, but stops for a moment to see how I'm doing. He wishes me success and adds, resuming his run:

"If you are accepted in the orchestra, you have a chance to get out!"

The sun manages to tear through the thick clouds. The ray of heat that penetrates me seems to be a good omen. But at once my heart freezes. Two men pass by me carrying a stretcher on which an inert body is stretched out, naked, livid, almost purple, arms dangling and face tensed in a hideously smiling grimace. It is the first corpse I've ever seen. Alas! It won't be the last!

"You have a chance to get out!" said the hairdresser to me. I'm willing to trust him. I chase away my pessimism and, courageously, I move towards barracks 15.

## III. FIRST SOUNDS

}

Maybe with time, I would get used to these violent transitions. But for the moment I'm all upset and dazzled by the spectacle that unfolds before my eyes.

From the threshold of barracks 15, I see a watertight partition that rises about ten meters from the entrance and separates this part from the rest of the building. On this partition, as on the other walls, many musical instruments are hung in the order of their dimensions. I can see copper basses, trombones, horns, trumpets, saxophones, clarinets, and two flutes, one large and one small. In a corner, a string double bass is leaning against the wall. In another, a bass drum and complete drum kit. Accordions and violin boxes are carefully arranged on several boards set up for this purpose. A second place holds stacks of sheet music and music paper. The brass instruments are well polished and reflect the sun's rays entering through the open door and through the cracks in the walls.

I immediately recognize the two imposing men who called me a few hours earlier. The one who spoke to me is sitting at a table, writing. The other is reading a book. In addition, three men are standing in the barracks and appear to be, with the other two, the staff of this "office." One of them, thin and frail, is bent over a dismembered accordion. In front of him is a small table with many tools of different sizes, as well as watches, an alarm clock, a small scale, and other miscellaneous objects. A small nervous and shabby creature is busy, near a red stove, frying sausage and potatoes whose aroma tickles my nostrils unbearably. Finally, a third man, wearing glasses, is looking at music sheets spread out in front of him and making annotations.

My greeting is met by an icy silence that is not very encouraging. These men hardly noticed my entrance. In any case, none of them deigns to interrupt their work. I stay for a long time in the doorway, not knowing what to say, much less what to do. Moving forward timidly, I stop in the middle of the room and contemplate one after the other these enigmatic individuals, their skulls closely shaved and shining like a well-kept parquet floor. With the exception of the little cook, they are all clean, elegant, distinguished and disturbing to the utmost. From time to time, the man with glasses casts an expressionless glance at me, a glance that I vainly try to find benevolent.

The cook has finished frying the dish. He pours it into a huge white bowl and respectfully places it in front of the man with the silver lyre, along with a large piece of white bread, a whiteness I hadn't seen in years. The man begins to eat greedily. I turn my head away to swallow my saliva.

Suddenly, a saxophone is brandished under my nose.

"Play it!" orders the man. "And quickly!"

I don't even have time to check if the reed or the mouthpiece is set to my use. I begin to play mechanically some kind of line.

"Enough!" I'm told at once.

The man with glasses then slips under my eyes a piece of music to decipher. There again, I barely have time to emit a few sounds of this music with such ease that one would think that it was chosen with the aim of encouraging my admission.

"That's enough!"

And the music is taken away from me as abruptly as it had appeared to me.

Leaving aside the frying attendant, who is now busy sweeping the room, the four men talk to each other in German. My fate is being decided and my anxiety grows as the interview goes on. Finally, the consultation is over and the one who seems to be the puppet master of the silver lyre figure approaches me and beckons me to follow him. Am I to understand that I have been accepted? Dragging myself behind my companion, I try to question him.

## III. FIRST SOUNDS

"Yes, you will do an internship, on a trial basis," he answers me with some impatience. "You'd better not celebrate too quickly. Just shut up, and you'll see."

After an hour, full of new formalities and various ablutions, I receive a decent striped suit that fits more or less, as well as clean underwear and a sweater; moreover, I put on shoes for the first time since I was stripped of my belongings. This unhoped-for change gives me back all of my courage. I do my best to carry out the orders of my new comrades conscientiously and despite the gruff and uninviting words I hear, to win their sympathy. I cannot explain why they are all so distant and where they get their air of superiority. Aren't we all prisoners, brothers of misfortune, and don't we have things to say to each other?

I courageously set to work. I am ordered to practice the saxophone in order to reacquire my somewhat neglected skill. I think I can do it in the barracks itself, but after a few scales and arpeggios I am told to go play outside. It disturbs the others.

Sitting on a mound of earth, close to the barracks, I tackle my instrument again, indifferent to the astonished looks of passers-by. I begin a series of exercises that should restore agility to my numb fingers.

A few meters away from me stands an endless row of huge cement posts, bent inward and joined by parallel barbed wire. Farther on, I see a similar fence, separated from ours by a road along which a car, loaded and dragged by prisoners, moves forward from time to time. Behind this second barbed-wire fence, strange creatures move about. Are these tiny creatures men? Are they children? Dressed in rags or used Soviet uniforms, they work with shovels or pickaxes, or carry stones or bricks in their crossed arms and seem to collapse under this excessive burden. One of these beings calls out to me and asks me to throw bread over the fences.

And it is then that I am stupefied that it is women who populate the camp next to mine! Yes, they are women, these little curled up monsters, with shaved heads, with skin as dry as old parchment, with a skeletal constitution, with a repulsive appearance! Several of them are now stationed in front of the barbed wire, making me understand that they are hungry, that they have neither clothes nor shoes. They show me their swollen feet and their skinny, naked thighs, all the while shouting at me:

"*Brot! Brot!*" (Bread! Bread!)

A German uniform appears on the road. The female ghosts disperse.

I relentlessly continue my scales and arpeggios.

# IV. QUATUOR

For several days I have been spending my time working on my saxophone and performing, during my brief moments of leisure, chores of all kinds. These chores are imposed on me, one after the other, by my new comrades. The little cook, the chattiest of the group, sometimes comes outside to find me for a rather friendly talk, but always with this air of superiority of which I seek in vain the reason. He makes it his duty to initiate me to the discipline of the orchestra, putting his care into deploying a whole system of education. It is thanks to Alix—that's the name of the little cook—that I now know what goes on in the orchestra, what our work consists of and—what interests me more particularly— the identities of the four men who were there the day I first entered the barracks where they sit almost in permanence.

The man with the lyre is, as I immediately thought, our music director, Franz Kopka. He's of dubious nationality; he claims to be German, but in reality he is of half-Czech, half-Polish origin. He wears a red triangle, as do all political prisoners, but everyone wonders, given the vileness and insignificance of his personage, what kind of criminal political activity he might have engaged in. Apart from that, one also wonders by what strange combination of circumstances he has been appointed music director. It seems that he is an absolute nullity on this point. It is whispered that he entered the service as a simple drummer, hardly knowing how to read music. Hated by all musicians and, in general, all the comrades of the camp, the SS tolerate him because of his nationality. But his professional inadequacy is the cause of many incidents that often lead to corporal punishments that the musicians are sometimes forced to share with him, in accordance with camp law.

If Alix speaks pejoratively about Kopka, he is, on the contrary, full of praise when it comes to his three acolytes, and especially to Heinz Lewin, a remarkable musician as well as luthier and clockmaker.

According to Alix, instead of mentioning the instruments Heinz plays, it is easier to say those he does not play. While of German origin, Heinz was arrested in France and deported here. At the moment, he is absorbed in the reconstruction of an accordion found in pieces in who knows where. He is said to be able to restore any damaged musical instrument. He knows, deeply, all the precise handiwork. In addition to his duties as a musician, he is quasi-officially responsible for repairing all the watches in the camp.

Lucien—that's the name of the one who called me a few days ago—is Kopka's most trusted man. A mediocre musician, he won Kopka's sympathy with his bawdy stories of love affairs, with his imposing physical appearance and, above all, with his exceptional gift of making fanciful pornographic drawings in series, which, by the way, are the delight of the SS. Lucien is, in fact, the only musician in the orchestra for whom Kopka feels a sincere sympathy, both personal and professional. The truth is that Lucien, who plays the violin and saxophone passably, excels in the kind of cabaret music that Kopka loves. Kopka often asks Lucien to play for him on his own. At each of his meals, Kopka always makes a point of leaving, with tender solicitude, his protégé the bottom of his white bowl to finish it. When the conductor of the orchestra is absent from the barracks, it is Lucien who is in charge of maintaining order and discipline among the musicians. But the authority of the latter, as well as that of Kopka himself, stops when it comes to pure musical technique. At this point, another figure emerges, that of André,[2] the man with glasses.

André is the real complete musician, and the entirety of his competence is revealed at each opportunity. Without a piano—in fact, we don't have one—he is able to harmonize and orchestrate any piece of music, often making do with a vocal line that is provided

---

2. This is Simon Laks. See above, p. 13, Footnote 1.

to him. Or, if a vocal line is not available, reconstructing the music from memory. He is in charge of writing all the orchestrations for our music, directing the rehearsals, and working out all the details of the performance. He is the real animator of our musical activity and it is thanks to his efforts that the orchestra can maintain its credibility with the Germans. Kopka does not like him, and this is because of his own inferiority, of which he is perfectly aware. André, on the other hand, does not like his conductor any better, but the camp hierarchy forces him to show him respectful obedience. All the musicians know that André is the only one with the skills of a conductor and that Kopka's role should have been limited to beating the drum. But Kopka is Aryan and German, while André is Jewish; that counts above all else.

The relationships between these four men are quite complex. On the one hand, they are determined by their respective functions. Kopka is the absolute master of our commando. He has the right to dismiss, at any time, with or without pretext, any musician. If he is sometimes careful not to use this privilege, it is primarily to maintain his personal situation, which can only last as long as there are musicians in his orchestra. However, another consideration, much more essential, comes into play for each of us: it is the degree of seniority in the camp, which is provided by the numbers tattooed on our arms. Those who have been in the camp for a long time have lower numbers than those who have just arrived. The first ones enjoy, a priori, indisputable advantages. The others, disdainfully called "millionaires," are relegated to the background. The old ones have the right to bully the "millionaires," to make them perform chores for their personal needs, to beat them, to punish them, in short, to degrade them without their being able to protest. Kopka, a German, number 11,000, and a music director to boot, is practically taboo. Only the SS could lay a hand on him. Lucien and André belong to the same generation of 49,000; Heinz: 74,000; Alix: 103,000; and finally, myself: 130,000. In this case, I am the "millionaire."

How could I not understand now this air of superiority that my colleagues and even this Alix take on, even though he only arrived at the camp three weeks before me? I now find it almost natural that my comrades are on a first-name basis with me, whereas I do not dare to allow this freedom with regard to them.

Alix also provides me with the explanation of the easy song that I was given to decipher during my entrance exam. The three comrades who made me undergo it come from France. They exploited Kopka's ignorance, which is often used to get another Frenchman into the music business. I highly appreciate this gesture of solidarity and I repent of having held a grudge against them for their attitude towards me. This is undoubtedly a purely external aspect of their personality, one that the conditions of the camp have made them adopt.

In spite of my expectations, my condition is not improved in any way by my admission to the orchestra. As in the past, a liter of soup and a ration of bread with a piece of sausage, margarine or a spoonful of marmalade, are allocated to me daily. I am constantly hungry and, when the food is distributed, I devour my share in one go, not having the will to save a little for the next morning. So I am fasting from the time I get up —which is at half past four —until noon.

Alix's situation is less bad, because he receives, for his services as a cook, his boss's share of the soup, which Kopka disdains.

I still do not know where Kopka gets the income from foodstuffs that allows him to do his own cooking. The fact is that he often has sausage and margarine in abundance, sometimes also meat, semolina, saccharine and even granulated sugar.

Alix also told me that the three acolytes of our chef also eat better than most musicians. They apparently have their own ways of raising their standard of living. Heinz, by repairing watches; Lucien,

## IV. QUATUOR

by monetizing his talents as a musician and designer of obscenities. André, finally, knows several foreign languages thoroughly and profits from the lessons he gives. Who is their clientele? A mystery!

From time to time, incidents occur in connection with these "private" activities. Kopka claims that the three privileged people are abusing his indulgence by indulging in prohibited trades and thus exposing him to substantial liability to the authorities. Indeed, all traffic is strictly forbidden and severely punished. But no one is fooled by Kopka's perfidious maneuvers, for he only wants to be granted a good part of his subordinates' earnings, the price of his silence. Thus, these discussions always end up being settled and nothing transpires outside.

In principle, we play twice a day: in the morning, when the commandos leave, and in the evening, when they return to camp. Between these two services, the musicians are employed in various outdoor jobs. They return at noon to eat their soup, go back to work and return half an hour before the other inmates, to prepare for the evening musical service. They are not free to relax until after roll call, which takes place at six o'clock and sometimes lasts an hour or more.

Only the four music masters remain in the barracks—the others must go to work. They only leave to play or for "business." As for Alix, his function as cook being illegal, he hides behind the authority of Kopka. Kopka sometimes keeps him in the hut, sometimes he, especially when he runs out of food, sends Alix to work with the others. Kopka himself is often absent during the day. Nobody knows exactly where he goes. Sometimes he comes back, pockets or cradle loaded with victuals and then gives the order, either to Alix, or to Lucien, to prepare him a succulent dish. It also happens that he comes back empty-handed, looking sheepish, and then he settles down, furious, to read a German detective novel, exchanged for another book, or he bravely starts to copy a few measures of a musical score, never used afterwards.

The number of our orchestra is, counting myself, thirty-five. I see very little of my other comrades because, not yet being officially assigned to the music, I sleep in my old barracks and I am obliged to present myself there also at roll call. I am therefore often alone, with my eternal saxophone, on which I continue to struggle to give satisfaction to my "superiors."

I'm looking forward to putting an end to these solitary exercises and to go out with the others, in order to have the certainty of being effectively incorporated. Not daring to speak to Kopka without having been challenged by him, I take the liberty of expressing my impatience to his close collaborators. For some time now, I have been talking to at least one of them every day, and they have become a little less haughty towards me. They make me understand, by somewhat confused hints, that I don't have to hurry and envy others, and that I'm good where I am.

Insensitive to these "fatherly" advices, I can hardly contain my joy when one evening Kopka calls me to him and, after a short conversation with André, encourages me to go, from the next day on, to work with the others.

That same evening, I am transferred to barracks 5, where all the musicians sleep.

The work that awaits me there does not worry me much. I am full of courage and strength. And I am all absorbed by the change in my condition, which translates for me into being officially admitted, as a musician, to the commando "*Lagerkapelle*."

# V. AUBADE

It is not yet daylight. The electric lamps on top of the curved cement poles surrounding our camp shine with their dull radiance as we leave the barracks with our instruments. A light rain, which we barely feel, is reflected in the glow of the lamps.

Five of us line up in the central aisle. Franz Kopka stands a little in front, with a baton in his hand. In the first row there are the five trumpets, then the other instruments come next. In last place there is the bass drum, flanked by the cymbal and the drum. To complete our formation there are two rows of violins which can't be played while walking so the musicians will follow with their cases under their arms.

All around us are gathered the more or less numerous groups of the different commandos. Many are standing between the barracks, others on the edges of the main alley, others still in the rather large space between the barracks and the entrance to the camp.

"Forward, march!" the leader calls out in a thunderous voice, and the column begins to move. As soon as we start moving, the drum starts a roll whose aim is to give rhythm to our steps and which, joined later by the bass drum and the cymbals, degenerates into a turbulent cadence. This is the signal for the attack of a German march, whose name has been shouted to us in the meantime.

Disturbed by this process in which I have not been initiated, I mechanically play my saxophone. I note with terror that the others play by heart and I am engulfed by despair for not knowing a single note of the march executed. In fact, I can hardly hear it, because the music is completely overpowered by the deafening rhythm of the drums. This rhythmic and monotonous motif is familiar to me. I had already perceived it in the distance, a few days before, and it is well engraved in my memory: two spaced blows, then three close blows, two blows, then three blows, two, three, two, three…

We walk for a few minutes, joyfully cheered on our way by the people with yellow armbands who are busy arranging their men in fives, and we arrive at the place where the music stands are located. Kopka gives the signal to stop by raising and lowering his baton with a sharp gesture. The musicians rush to their seats. I find mine with difficulty. Music notebooks are quickly distributed to us; the violinists take out their instruments. I open my music notebook, ready to start the first piece. But it is still dark and the light coming from the electric lamps does not allow us to distinguish the notes. My neighbor, the flutist—a Greek who speaks French very well—calms my fervor by explaining to me that the commandos will only start to come out when the day will have dawned and that in the meantime we are going to play something other than marches.

It is quite cold and we have only our suits on, unlike our leader who wears his short overcoat decorated with the silver lyre. Kopka seems to be in a good mood, joking with the yellow armband wearers who have approached us and who are offering him cigarettes. He cheerfully gives us the title of a piece and raises his baton. The rain increases little by little.

The orchestra starts a tango that I do not know any more than the march previously played. I don't see the point of pretending to know it and I put down my instrument. But Kopka notices it, comes to me, and slaps me without preamble, which causes a general hilarity. He shouts:

"Idiot, play!"

I am about to answer that I do not know this music, but a blow to my knee by my neighbor makes me realize that it would be even more of a blunder. I resolve to mime the tango as best I can, worried about what might happen next. I can feel my leader's scrutinizing gaze on me, but suddenly an unexpected intervention from the Germans puts an end to my torment.

## V. AUBADE

A guttural order from one of the SS guards on the other side of the wire makes us stop our music. Kopka rushes back to where he came from and stands at attention. I hear a few words being shouted. Kopka comes back like a galloping horse and, addressing this time the trumpets, orders a new title. And I hear, to my astonishment, a jazz piece that reminds me of the good bands I used to applaud when I was free. Only a part of the orchestra joins in, they are obviously the best musicians. They seem to excel in this genre. Kopka is now in his element. He has put down his baton and conducts only with the two fingers of each hand. His knees wiggle from right to left, seeming to imitate the international stars. He seems to take the dizzying improvisations of his disciples in stride and seems to believe, judging by his blissful satisfaction, that he deserves all the credit.

It is almost daylight when the piece ends in a din of applause and cheers. The main door is now wide open. An SS guard shouts:

"C'mon! Music!"

And we attack our first march, this time from the scores spread out on our music stands. Immediately, the columns of prisoners begin to march in front of us, one after the other, out of the camp. In the first row of each column stands a man with a yellow armband bearing this title painted in black Gothic letters: "Kapo." As he passes the group of SS men stationed at the gate, he shouts out the number of his group, at the same time as they all tip their caps as one man, in accordance with the rite. As the rows pass by, the SS men count them and write them down carefully.

The rain becomes heavier and soaks our scores, blurring the notes written in ink. Kopka signals to the violins to put away their instruments and to pick up the music notebooks. We still have to play by heart, which means for me the resumption of my pantomime. The drums are still playing their two spaced blows, three close blows, and the men are still marching and tipping their caps in front of the SS who are counting them.

And we play our marches, tirelessly, under pouring rain. I am soaked to the bone and my saxophone is dripping on all sides. It's a good thing I don't know what's being played, because I wouldn't be able to get a single note out of my saxophone anyway. Besides, most of the musicians are struggling with their flooded instruments. Only the brass and the cymbals save the situation and hold on, as best they can, until the end.

The last commando has left. We stop playing and leave our places to quickly line up in the aisle. The drum ceremony starts again, followed by the bass drum and cymbals. We head back to our barracks to the sound of another cheerful march.

Once under cover, we carefully wipe down and put away our instruments. I wonder how I will be able to dry myself. Seeing Alix already fussing around his stove, I approach him to help him build the fire. However Kopka does not leave me time to carry out my plan.

"Quickly! Get out! To work!" he shouts at me. "I don't want to see anyone here!"

Without understanding what kind of work it is, I mechanically leave the barracks. Resigned, my comrades are already going up the central alley and I guess that they didn't have to be given any order to get going. They seem to be used to it and it must always be so.

Alix is not delayed in joining us. Only the four privileged ones remained in the shelter.

# VI. BROKEN CADENCES

Following my comrades who are numb with cold like me, I arrive at the end of the camp where two horse-drawn carriages are parked near the barbed wire. Our detachment, composed of thirty men, is divided into two groups, each assigned to a carriage. These vehicles are large and apparently very unwieldy, and seem to require at least two animals to move them. In this case, it is us who replace the hitching animals. Fourteen of us handle the truck, the fifteenth acting as supervisor. He has been designated by our music director. Two men stand at the tiller, six take ropes or wires attached to the hooks fixed to the car, the others push from the sides or from the bottom.

The baritone player is our team leader. He is a strong man, recently arrived at the camp; a bad comrade, a bad musician, but an excellent trainer. The car is badly sunk in the sticky ground and we have trouble starting it. Our supervisor, equipped with a stick, yells and knocks, but refrains from giving us a hand. The car does not want to move.

At this moment, an SS appears in the distance. As if stimulated by a mysterious force, the car moves again and we can take it to the central alley, where our task is significantly lightened, as this alley forms a pronounced incline. Arrived safely at the edge of the camp, we undergo the checking of numbers, as the protocol demands it, then find ourselves outside.

We are in muddy, hilly terrain, strewn with ruts and puddles. Multiple obstacles make our journey difficult. We have to double our efforts to push the car when we go up a hill, and to hold it when it is on a slope. The wheels sink at any moment into the slippery mud and we have to pull them out with our bare hands clutching the spokes. Every meter is a new burden, the shouts and the blows start again; sometimes they come from our team leader, sometimes from the German soldiers we pass. The accumulating rain increases the difficulty of the work. I am completely wet and I don't know anymore if it is the rain or the sweat that is the main cause. We are up to our knees in mud and our pants are filthy. More and more often the terrain presents insurmountable obstacles. Some of us give up when we could have succeeded with a collective effort.

No one knows what time it might be. Every now and then, I hear one of my neighbors say:

"It still isn't noon?"

Noon! That means rest for an hour and the distribution of soup. The time has seemed so long that we feel that noon must not be far away. Perhaps it is eleven o'clock, or even a quarter past eleven?

We arrive in sight of a stone quarry. About fifty men of another commando are working there digging holes and extracting large stones, of which a huge quantity already litter the ground. We have to load our car with them, using the shovels that lie nearby.

We are now in an open plain. A terrible wind has added to the rain. Not having enough shovels, we take turns loading the car. It is only while working that one is the least cold. The non-workers warm themselves as best they can, by stamping their feet in the mud or by hitting their arms energetically against their shoulders.

The car is finally full and we must now drive it to our camp to unload it. We are afraid that we will not be back by noon and will miss our soup. In spite of our exhaustion, we have to make an effort disproportionate to that which we have previously made to move the car filled with stones. They are, multiplied by ten, the same pushes, the same shouts, the same blows from all sides.

We arrive at the camp at the end, dead tired, and we start to unload the truck. One of our companions goes away for a moment to ask if the lunch is already distributed. He comes running back and shouts to us:

"It is only half past eight!"

## VI. BROKEN CADENCES

That day, we make five similar trips, there and back: three in the morning and two in the afternoon.

Weary from work that would have exhausted beasts of burden, we return with our legs wobbling, our clothes, hands and faces covered with mud. We barely have time to put our vehicle away after unloading when Kopka, who has been watching for our return, orders us to clean ourselves up in a flash, because it is time for the commandos to return and we have to go and play.

How to get cleaned up? I watch the others do it. Using bits of wood, penknives, and spoons, they remove the scabs stuck to their clothes, which they then wash with water taken from stagnant ponds, of which there are many inside the camp. The result is poor, but I imitate their game and I am almost as presentable as my friends.

Before the instruments are distributed to us, Kopka gives us a detailed inspection.

"You lazy bastards," he yells, "How do you look? Look at me and look at yourselves!"

Indeed, the comparison is well to his advantage. He is clean, elegant, well dressed, and his boots are polished. We look miserable, in spite of our efforts to clean ourselves up. But we don't have time to do better. We are called to play.

And, once again, the triumphant sounds of our military marches resonate. In front of us the parade of prisoners begins again, but now in the opposite direction, and how different from that of this morning!

With the exception of the Kapos and the team leaders, the men walk with difficulty, their heads and shoulders slumped. Some bear the marks of blows, others support those who cannot walk alone. At the end of almost every column, inanimate men lie on wheelbarrows or carts, or on improvised stretchers, dragged or carried by the less weak. Sometimes, and especially when they are more numerous and therefore more difficult to count, these inert bodies are thrown to the ground without care and reloaded after verification. For the number of prisoners returning, alive or dead, must be exactly equal to the number declared in the morning at the exit.

The show obviously lasts much longer than in the morning. Until the last commando has returned, we play our jolly marches.

After roll call, which lasts about an hour, we each get a piece of bread and margarine. It is seven o'clock. We can, in principle, have our time until nine o'clock, bedtime.

I swallow my ration, gluttonously. I don't have the courage to exchange a word with my bedmate; I just want to lie down and forget as soon as possible the day I have just lived.

Plunged into a complete annihilation of body and soul, I wonder how many days it will be possible for me to endure such a regimen.

# VII. DUO

Lying on my bunk, before lights out, I try in vain to ignore the comings as well as the hubbub in the barracks. I recapitulate, in my mind, the heavy moments of the past day. A terror comes over me as I try to imagine what the next few days will be like. I look with envy at the prisoners who, unlike me, are strongly built, and have pink chubby cheeks from eating large slices of bread and bacon, and I don't understand how they can access this food. No wonder they look so good. Then, I contemplate the many skeletal figures that pass me by, who, as I did, must have eaten their ration in one sitting. How long will it take me to look like them?

Suddenly, I see André heading my way. Despite my feelings, I close my eyes, pretending to sleep. A "How's it going?" makes me open them again. But André is already moving away, to enter the corridor where his bed is.

Without knowing why, this small greeting without emotion shakes me to my core. Mechanically, as if pushed by a spring, I jump up and there I am right behind him.

He doesn't realize that I have followed him and I take a chance by greeting him with "Sir!" as he begins to unbutton his pants, while turning his back. He finally sees me and, while taking off his jacket, says to me, with a tone of rudeness that hurts:

"Do not call me 'sir!' What is it?"

I am dumbfounded. I can't find the words to answer him. And, deep down, do I even know what I want to tell him? Can't he guess it? Can't he see my distress?

He continues to undress quietly, pulls off his sweater and as his head disappears into the knitting, I hear his voice muffled by the wool, resume:

"Come on! Speak!"

I stammer with difficulty:

"Uh... Sir..."

"My name is André!" he interrupts brutally.

"Oh! Mister André... I can't take it anymore!"

I feel that something collapses inside me and I burst into tears.

Suddenly, a loud slap strikes my face. My crying stops as if by magic. My cheek is on fire and I wake up from my stupor. A silence follows. While I instinctively caress my cheek, André removes his pants and enters his bed. While arranging his numerous covers, he continues:

"You can't take it anymore? Well, it's simple. Look over there, yes, the barbed wire. They are loaded with high voltage current. Go ahead, try to touch them and it will be over!"

I don't understand anything he's saying, but to my amazement, the harshness of what he's saying seems to me to be the most disinterested of solicitudes.

"How long have you been here?" he continues in the same hurtful tone. "Answer me!"

"Eleven days..."

"I've been here eighteen months. How many days of outside work have you already done?"

"Today was the first."

"And the gentleman is already tired? I've done sixty. That was in 1942. And not as a musician!"

He emphasizes the word "musician" with great disdain, as if he himself were not one. He probably wants me to understand that the musicians' outside work is nothing compared to that of the other commandos.

"Do you have any idea where you are? You are alive, what more do you want? Others are in ashes. You know that, right? So what are you complaining about? You're involved with music where you might have the chance to scrape by a little longer than anywhere else. Did you get a sweater? So did I, but it's the first time since I've been here. Tomorrow you'll be getting a coat and gloves, and last winter we had none.

He pauses for a moment, as if chasing away a bad memory...

"I'm going to sleep," he adds wearily, "so should you. And be careful, don't cry. We don't cry here, or we'd never stop... I'll prove to you when the time comes that our camp is a sanatorium compared to what it was a year and a half ago... Go!" he finishes, turning over to sleep.

I take a few steps towards my bed. I see that I am as helpless as before. The lecture that André has just given me has hardly sunk in. A sanatorium? Is he making fun of me? I see in my mind the car full of stones that I will have to tackle again tomorrow, the day after tomorrow and the following days...

André's voice calling me back distracts me from my thoughts. I come back to him and find him cutting a big slice of bread that he hands me with a double ration of sausage.

"Oh! Mr. André... thank you..." are the only words I murmur almost in a breath, taking the generous offering. With a gesture of impatience, he lets me know how little importance he attaches to his generosity.

"Tell me," he says, as if to change the subject, "What else do you know how to do, apart from music?"

"I know how to tinker... I sew a little..."

"Good!" he notes, after a short reflection. "Now, let me sleep. And I warn you that I'll smash your face in if you say "sir" again!"

"Good night... André... and thank you again."

I don't know if he heard me because, without giving an answer, he has already wrapped himself in his blankets over his head.

I am transformed. Suddenly, all my courage comes back. The car loaded with stones, the rain, the work, the blows, nothing frightens me anymore. I can only hear André's rough voice now and I wonder if it was a dream.

But the precious gift I hold in my hands is palpable proof of the reality of the scene I have just experienced.

# VIII. SOLI

My neighbor in the orchestra, the flutist, is also my neighbor in the bunk I occupy at the lowest of the three floors of the frames that serve, at the same time, as our lodging and bed.

He is a graduate of the University of Toulouse as a medical doctor and has obtained a prize as a flutist from the Conservatory of the same city. The fact of belonging to our music did not make him neglect his first vocation. He has managed, I don't know how, to make himself a small medical kit hidden in a flat cardboard box that he keeps under his bench. Given the scrapes that most of us get during the work, the Doctor—that's what we call him—has built up quite a clientele, not only among the musicians but also among the other occupants of the barracks. The care he gives us earns him small rewards in kind, and his carton contains, besides tincture of iodine, hydrogen peroxide, bandages and some substantial provisions.

The Doctor and the accordionist Michel, his compatriot[3], who arrived at the camp at the same time as him, form a couple of inseparable friends. I often see the two of them, standing at the barbed wire fence from which one can observe the women's camp. The Doctor has his daughter there and Michel his two sisters. Whenever they can, they wait for them to appear, to exchange a few words or to throw them some food over the barbed wire. Their wait is often in vain.

The violinist Dimitri, also Greek, is in the same compartment as me, on the other side of the Doctor. He is an inveterate smoker. While most musicians are deprived of tobacco and have to resort to extraordinary means to get some, Dimitri smokes constantly. He is unparalleled in his ability to solicit the last few puffs from the privileged few who are just finishing their cigarettes. As soon as he

---

3. It is certainly Michel Assael, born in Thessaloniki in 1918 and died in 2006. [Ed. note]

sees one of them, he inserts himself two steps away from them, takes out a wooden cigarette smoker that he made himself and manipulates it innocently in his fingers until the smoker has noticed the maneuver and gratifies him with the last centimeter of his cigarette. Even though he doesn't know any other language than Greek, Dimitri makes himself understood by everyone, thanks to his mimicry and his gestures. And it is rare that he does not get the desired cigarette butt. When we go out with the car, Dimitri has the same place every time. He would even fight to keep it. From this place, he has the chance to be the first to see the cigarette butts that can be found on the roads we are walking. As soon as an object resembling a cigarette butt is in sight, he leaves the car in a hurry to grab it, notwithstanding the risk of being run over or punished. On the way back to the camp, he has his little iron box full of cigarette butts.

One of the most remarkable instrumentalists in our ensemble is undoubtedly young Henri. A violinist of prodigious technique, he plays by heart all the concert pieces in the repertoire of the great soloists. He entered the camp at the age of fourteen, and thanks to his talent, he was able to overcome all the first tests. The authorities surrounded him with a real protection, showering him with gifts of all kinds as a reward for his concerts.

But the atmosphere of detention created and developed in him a casualness and an uncontrolled carelessness that transformed him into a true musical Gavroche. As soon as he saw me for the first time, he befriended me and promised me all kinds of things. This lasted three days. Now, I no longer exist for him. The Doctor, seeing my disappointment, tells me that Henri's friendships never last long and that he proceeds in this way every time a new musician enters the orchestra.

Henri's ability to monetize his musical abilities has led him to engage in a huge traffic, of which theft and lies are far from being excluded. Time and time again, his close friends notice the ravages of their bags, and no one is unaware of the perpetrator, although Henri has never let himself be caught in the act. And then, suddenly, he has a crisis of generosity so he distributes his wealth everywhere. Sometimes, the beneficiaries recognize, among this prodigality, the objects from which they were robbed a few days before. However, no one ever thinks of holding a grudge against him, because he only has to take his violin to be forgiven for his sins.

Henri is accompanied by the best of our accordionists, whom we call Bronek. As a soldier in the Polish army, he was wounded in the knee by shrapnel, which made his leg stiff. This defect did not prevent him from ending up in our camp and I think that he, more than any of us, owes his life to his presence in the music. He is practically incapable of any physical effort and is always forced to hide so as not to go out to work with us. Although he is not always able to do this, we help him in every way possible to avoid these chores, which are very painful for him. We try to hide his infirmity. When we march to music, he is flanked by his two neighbors in the orchestra who, in this way, prevent him from being noticed too much.

The musical superiority of some of my colleagues only reinforces the already existing hierarchy due to their seniority. As a "millionaire" I have to suffer the whims, if not the commands, of almost all the musicians who do not fail, at every opportunity, to act authoritatively because they have a smaller number than I do. But I note, not without some satisfaction, that they in turn are subject to the authority of their elders and that this hierarchical ladder is getting longer and longer, culminating in the person of Franz Kopka, our conductor, master of our destiny.

However, like Kopka himself, we have an official superior, appointed by the German authorities from among the oldest prisoners, who is a sort of camp administrator. He is the *Lagerältester* Franz Danisch[4], whose very sight makes all the prisoners tremble. His origin is as dubious as Kopka's: half-Polish, half-German from Silesia, he was able to gain the trust of the SS as soon as he arrived, thanks to his numerous denunciations. His rapid rise to prominence is the eternal topic of conversation among the prisoners.

The Germans greatly appreciated the services Franz Danisch had rendered them by denouncing the slightest offence, so they appointed him head of the barracks so that he could better exercise his vigilance among the prisoners. The Germans decided to punish all barracks leaders with twenty-five strokes of the stick on the back of their legs. When Danisch's turn came, he refused to bend down and, addressing the SS who were present at the beatings, said the following:

"What do you mean, you want to beat me! And why? The incident that occurred was not the fault of the barracks leaders. Only your *Lagerältester* is responsible. He is not up to his task. Let me be appointed to this position and you will see that the slightest failure will not happen again! You will have a model camp that I will make for you in a few days!"

The Germans, stunned by this bold language coming from a prisoner, nevertheless accepted his challenge. They did not correct him and immediately appointed him to this honorary position.

Franz Danisch kept his promise. From the most miserable to the most privileged, all the inmates are terrified when he appears in the distance. He succeeded in doing what his predecessors had tried in vain to do: he militarized terror.

---

4. Born on October 4, 1902 in Chorzów, a merchant by profession, he was deported to Auschwitz on April 5, 1941 and registered under number 11182 as a common law prisoner and *Reichsdeutscher* (pure German). [Ed. note]

# IX. FRAGILE CONSONANCES

In the weeks following my first face-to-face contact with André, I am able to overcome my depression little by little. Physically, the irregular but substantial food support that he provides helps me endure the often-painful efforts that I continue to make periodically. Morally, it is the brief conversations I have with him that contribute to my improvement. Sometimes a simple phrase that he says to me in passing sustains me. Although he continues to keep his distance, I have the feeling that I have found in him a friend, a protector.

The day after our first colloquium, he manages to get me to stay in the barracks with the privileged few, to sew the pieces of cloth bearing our numbers on the winter coats that are distributed to the musicians. This takes my mind off the physical work. A few days later, the opportunity is renewed to proceed with the same operation, this time on the additional costumes that we received, destined to be put on only to play. These precious hours, taken away from outside work, also preserve my strength and delay the exhaustion. André also teaches me the art of acting at work in front of our supervisors, prisoners or SS, an art whose experience almost cost him his life on several occasions. In this way I learn, progressively, to furtively scan the immediate surroundings of the workplaces and to take advantage of the slightest moment of inattention from our executioners to relax from my efforts. "Spare your muscles, work with your eyes," he says constantly.

On the other hand, we are sometimes given less exhausting work, such as transporting clothes for disinfection, cleaning the interior of the camp, beautifying the surroundings of the barracks, etc... At other times, we are sent to the neighboring camps to transport or pick up planks or earth. Sunday, officially a day of rest, is not always a day of rest for us, although we prefer it to weekdays. Various chores are imposed on us on this day without any apparent necessity: carrying earth in our jackets that have been turned inside out, endless "lice calls," and multiple tasks of circumstance inside the camp.

Immutably we play mornings and evenings, in all kinds of weather, whether it is freezing, snowing or windy; it seems impossible for the Germans to envision the exit or re-entry of the commandos without our help. When it is foggy, the commandos do not go out until it has dissipated: fog favors escapes. We have to then stay for long hours playing entertaining tunes until the order to attack our marches is given.

To anyone who might glance at us, what a strange sight this company of musician-convicts must be, covered with a thick layer of snow, blowing furiously into their instruments to brighten up the grim procession of frozen men, skeletons and corpses! And yet, this spectacle becomes natural and familiar to all who take part in it, including myself.

It is only much later that, thanks to a trick of our leader, we will obtain the favor to postpone these painful exhibitions during severe weather.

Recently, Kopka has managed to get two regular rehearsals a week, but just in the afternoons. Before, these sessions only took place according to the goodwill and the mood of our superiors. The innovation of this reform was due to *Lagerführer* Schwarzhuber himself,[5] who had expressed the wish to hear us play some German operetta medleys and also his favorite aria *Heimat deine Sterne*—Homeland, Your Stars—which was very famous in Germany and taken from the famous Nazi propaganda film *Quax*.[6] In order to make

---

5. Commandant of the male camp from March 14, 1942 to September 10, 1944. [Ed. note]
6. *Quax der Bruchpilot* (Quax the crash pilot), 1941.

## IX. FRAGILE CONSONANCES

his wish possible, Schwarzhuber allows us to increase the number of copyists, which of course reduces the number of musicians working outside.

These two unheard-of favors, officially granted by the supreme authority of the camp, and which represents for the majority of us an unprecedented relief, unleashes the ill-contained fury of Franz Danisch, who has become the sworn enemy of music in general and of ours in particular. A sly conflict ensues, which soon degenerates into an almost open war, not between Franz Danisch and our music, which would have been natural, but between the prisoner Franz Danisch and the SS *Hauptsturmführer* Schwarzhuber, our commandant! And strange as it may seem, it is not always the latter who comes out on top. Danisch's argument is irrefutable: "I am responsible for the work done, I need manpower and not music copyists or rehearsals!" Thus, more than once, Commandant Schwarzhuber sees the development of his beloved song relegated to the background.

Franz Danisch! Franz Kopka! Two abject scum, two camp aristocrats, two tutors whom fate has sent me and whose teaching has helped me to perfect my education as a model prisoner! I feel an unspeakable embarrassment in immortalizing these two Franzes, so strangely mixed up in my memories!

In spite of the changes that our rehearsals sometimes undergo thanks to Danisch's assiduity, they nevertheless continue to take place quite regularly. These half-days of music are a real relaxation for all musicians. They are awaited with the same impatience as the time of the soup or the distribution of the rations. The work is carried out under the competent baton of André and under the high and useless supervision of Kopka, who never misses an opportunity to show his complete musical ignorance. He is always intervening at the wrong moment, which is a highly amusing gift for the real musicians of the orchestra who hold back, with difficulty, their laughter.

These sessions also help to bring me closer to those of my comrades whom I have not had the opportunity to meet until now. I realize that most of them lead a life as miserable, if not more so, than mine.

Of different nationalities, they exchange words in the most picturesque gibberish, sometimes in a friendly manner, sometimes arguing over the sharing of food. They manage, by any means available to them, to improve their poor diet. Some exchange their soup for sausage, sell it for cigarettes, and then buy the same soup back with the profit of a cigarette which they smoke or trade for a piece of bread. Others have friends or relatives in better positions than themselves who, from time to time, can give them a soup or a ration.

A different fate is reserved for the best elements of the orchestra, especially those who have the gift of entertaining the audience. With Kopka's support, they go to the private rooms of the Kapos and baton twirlers to entertain them. They go there two or three times a week in the evening after roll call and always return with packages containing food and cigarettes, thus arousing the envy of the others. The contents of these packets are unerringly shared with Kopka. In fact, these private music sessions are strictly forbidden by the rules—is there anything that is not?—and Franz Danisch goes to great lengths to track them down. The risk is therefore serious and the burden of responsibility is on both sides. It is not surprising that the benefits are equally shared.

These privileged musicians are seven or eight in number, always the same. Lucien is one of them, with his gypsy music in which he excels and his extraordinary fantasies which attract a crowd of devotees.

I never saw Heinz, nor André, participate in these sorts of escapades. Perhaps they don't possess that special gift of entertaining an easy audience with an easy repertoire; perhaps they would have done so if they were forced to, either by necessity or by order. One thing is certain: neither of them had any need to resort to this means of "earning a living," being sufficiently provided with all that a prisoner hardly dares to dream of. In addition to their well-stocked pantry, they both have custom-made striped suits, cinched at the waist, and their pants, widened at the bottom, always have a neat crease. Their heads get shaved every Saturday by a "private" barber, generously paid in cigarettes, which they hold in considerable quantities.

Heinz, as we already know, is a watchmaker, and what a watchmaker! Watches are everywhere in the camp and their number is always increasing. Where do they come from? I hardly dare to think about it. Every SS man, regardless of rank, every Kapo, every barracks leader, every inmate official, no matter how important—in short, every self-respecting inmate—has one or more watch bracelets. A watch—it's a kind of passport, a survival visa and an indisputable proof of a solid establishment in the camp.

Heinz is an excellent watchmaker and yet his customers repeatedly bring him their wristwatches, repaired only a few days before, often even the day before. The SS, the privileged prisoners known as "prominences," never miss an opportunity to hit their subordinates, and their watches break periodically. Our watchmaker is never short of work and his supply of victuals is always abundant. His activity as a watchmaker is carried out in full view of everyone, although it is "strictly forbidden" like everything else. The great art of the perfect prisoner is to show an apparent decency by hiding the evidence of the crime. I once saw the head of our barracks beat a poor man whom he had caught smoking during working hours. He beat the man, but made him understand that it was not because he had smoked, but because he had not pretended to hide his cigarette when he saw him coming.

Every time Heinz receives payment from his customers for his work as a watchmaker, Kopka receives a large percentage in the form of a "loan" that is never repaid, but this does not prevent him from making the eternal threat to turn him in to the Germans. He does the same with André.

It is confirmed that André supports himself by giving French and English lessons to some of the camp's senior officials. Among his students are the head cook, the canteen worker, and the head of the supply store. André's income is almost as large as that of the watchmaker. He is "paid" in sausages or whole loaves of bread, in potatoes, in semolina, in packets of margarine or cigarettes, often even in pâté and ham. It is with sincere emotion that I notice that André does not think only about himself. The first thing he obtains from the chef is an extra 25 liters of soup for the band every day, which significantly improves the diet of the poorest among us.

For some time now André has had an "aide-de-camp" of his own. He is a Russian prisoner of war, George, a bass player. He is devoted to him body and soul, as he has often told me. André saved his life by giving him extra food when he was admitted to the music room, totally exhausted. Every evening, after roll call, I see George peeling potatoes and onions in a corner of the barracks, cooking them and then frying them with margarine and slices of sausage. He thus obtains two large bowls of a tasty and nourishing dish. Four or five men benefit from this, including myself and sometimes Kopka, when he is short of victuals from his own source.

For Christmas 1943, we had to move out of rehearsal barracks 15 and take our instruments to barracks 5, where we are housed. A large area of these barracks, separated from the rest of the building by thick boards, became our *Musikstube* (music room) where our instruments are parked and where Kopka, André, Lucien, one or two "seasonal" copyists and the inevitable clockmaker usually sit. The rehearsals are now held here because, during working hours, there is no one else here except a few sick people authorized to stay. The musicians sit on

## IX. FRAGILE CONSONANCES

either side of the heating duct that divides the room in two along its length, and the conductor stands on the duct itself.

More and more often, I am allowed to stay in the *Musikstube*, either to sew or to clean the instruments. Alix is no longer Kopka's regular cook. He was replaced for a few days by Henri, who was in turn fired for almost starting a fire while he was cooking. And now it's George who is standing in.

My friendship with André seems to be growing stronger. I don't always get to the bottom of his thinking, and I often feel that my attentions bother him. But, if the form of his kindness rarely satisfies me, the essence of it is of primordial material help. I have almost regained my former strength, and when I am called upon to do some outside work, I can do my share of the work with relative ease.

I have noticed that once or twice a week André mysteriously goes away late at night. Perhaps it is for his lessons? In any case, the next day he gives me, confidentially, the latest political news and information from the front. He told me about the victory in Stalingrad in great detail. It was through him that I first learned that we could send news to our families. Much later, it was again he who told me about the assassination attempt on Hitler's life, before anyone in the camp knew about it.

Every piece of news he brings me is not only a proof of his friendship and trust, but also an encouragement for the future. But when I share with him my optimism, he looks at me with a mixture of kindness and indulgence, like a grown man watching a child play with a toy.

And my toy is the hope that one day I will get out of here alive, despite the ominous clouds hanging over our heads.

# X. MUSIC FIRST!

Kopka's absences become more and more frequent and prolonged. I believe that the Gestapo office in Auschwitz I is responsible for these trips, but I do not know the purpose. In any case, I am happy about this, as are all my comrades, because it is André who is responsible for leading us during these absences.

One afternoon Kopka, returning from one of his outings, proudly enters the barracks where we are rehearsing, and announces—to our great amazement—that he is going to be released! We congratulate him loudly and our joy is very sincere. However, Kopka is not fooled by our demonstration and throws out nastily:

"Ah, you think you'll be rid of me! Wait a minute, I haven't left yet!"

Openly and unintentionally, Kopka confesses what we all suspected. Deep down, this unexpected liberation is far from delightful for him. His pride is only fabricated. He doesn't really like to leave a good position in the camp to go to a hell. For no one is unaware, and Kopka least of all, that the few Germans liberated from the camp must join the German army and that this is the price of their liberation. Just think, to come down from the pedestal of music director to the rank of simple second class and to be directed, perhaps, to the Russian front where the battle is raging! It would be better to stay here, as long as possible, and quietly enjoy the comfortable life that his "protégés" provide him!

We soon learn that Kopka will be released only after a month of preventive medical observation. He seems delighted and, on several occasions, expresses his happiness among his immediate entourage:

"At least that's something, the war might be over by then."

This delay momentarily disappoints us, but we are soon rewarded with another pleasant surprise: Kopka is now assigned to the quarantine barracks and officially exempted from work!

## X. MUSIC FIRST!

As an immediate result of this measure, we see less and less of him among us, and while he continues to sit in the music room as a freeloader—his personal income having suddenly fallen to zero—his situation no longer allows him to take an active interest in music.

From that moment on, André is virtually our conductor, although he does not wear the silk armband that still adorns Kopka's sleeve. The results of his leadership are immediately apparent.

Not only do the musicians have a sincere sympathy for the new conductor, but they are happy to feel that they are finally in expert hands. André has taken advantage of the relative independence he now enjoys to enrich our repertoire with good music, as much as naturally possible. Although we are obliged to play only German music, we work, without daring to perform them publicly, on French, Czech, Polish and Russian works, transcribed from memory for our heterogeneous ensemble. We work with piety and devotion, always on the alert, fearing an untimely visit and ready to attack, if necessary, any German tune.

Independently of this intimate activity, our orchestra is making brilliant progress and, even when we perform the traditional marches, we receive many testimonies of satisfaction from the Kapos and even the SS. But the most extraordinary and unexpected reaction comes from Franz Danisch.

One afternoon, while walking along the path, I see Kopka coming in the opposite direction. Unshaven, noticeably slimmed down, huddled into himself, he is the image of abandonment and carelessness. At the same time, André appears at the threshold of our barracks, clean, impeccable and looking elegant. Suddenly, I hear the thunderous voice of Danisch, who has apparently been contemplating the two men for a while:

"Kopka, what a sight you are, nothing like a *Kapellmeister*, aren't you ashamed? Look," he adds, pointing to André, "what a real

*Kapellmeister* looks like! With him, the music sounds great! It's a pleasure now to watch the commandos marching to work!"

André himself cannot believe it. Would Danisch finally declare peace with the musicians?

Since this event, Kopka, exasperated by the evidence of his downfall, has not ceased to engage in clandestine activity, with the aim of destroying André, without ceasing to be supported by him. Then one day Kopka disappears. We learn that he is now obliged to stay in bed because of a mysterious illness. Twice a day he sends a messenger to ask for food. But after several times satisfying these inexplicable demands, André has agreed with Heinz and Lucien to stop this useless generosity, preferring to share the surplus with comrades who deserve it more.

A few days passed without a hitch. Then, suddenly, Kopka reappears.

A hideous corpse, he strides into the music room where the usual trio is sitting, with George busy cooking a delicious meal. Sure that something extraordinary is about to happen between these men, I approach the window looking into the room with a few of my comrades.

We see Kopka shaking like a lunatic, shouting and threatening everyone with his fist brandished in the air. He seems to be giving André an order that André refuses to carry out. Then, with an unpredictable gesture, he pushes George away from the stove, grabs the dish that is cooking, throws it on the floor, after which he approaches the table where the watchmaker is working and, with his arm, throws everything in the air. Now we hear him shouting in a mad rage at André:

"I'm going to tell the *Lagerführer* everything! You're going to come with me to his house right now!"

André quietly strides to his coat, puts it on, opens the door, and ironically bows to let Kopka pass.

## X. MUSIC FIRST!

We are breathless from the quarrel and wonder how it will end. The two men are indeed heading for the SS building. No doubt they will appear before our Commander Schwarzhuber.

I am terribly worried about André. Between Kopka, Aryan, German, almost army soldier number 11,000 and André, Jew, 49,000, can the outcome of the arbitration leave a shadow of doubt?

The twenty minutes during which we repair the ravages wrought by Kopka seem like an eternity. We are in the grip of extreme nervousness.

André and Kopka finally appear at the end of the avenue. We all stand in front of the barracks to see them coming.

Kopka, looking very sheepish, drags himself along behind André, who is walking happily and is getting further and further ahead of him. Some of us rush to meet André, asking:

"So what?"

André shows us a few shreds of black silk that he is holding in his hand. We recognize the old armband, with the silver lyre, which until recently adorned Kopka's left arm. We learn that Kopka was judiciously slapped by our commander, who also tore off his armband and gave it to André, symbolically naming him the official music director.

We never saw our former *Kapellmeister* again. It was not given to him, however, to increase the strength of the German army. We were to learn later that he had died, abandoned by all, even by those who called themselves his friends. His death had occurred the day before he was to be released.

# XI. MODULATIONS

All the musicians have expressed, collectively and individually, their satisfaction with André's appointment. No one is as happy and proud as I am. I keep telling him how delighted I am, for him and for all of us, to see him finally in his true place. I wish he would lighten up and share my joy and optimism!

Yet, despite his customary impassivity, André sometimes reveals his true feelings, suggesting that he is satisfied with his present condition. He is obviously happy to be able to engage in a much wider range of musical activity than before and also to contribute to making the lives of his musicians more bearable. Along with his purely musical duties, another delicate and thankless task now falls to him: that of distributing the outside work among the members of his "commando." Taking advantage of Franz Danisch's good disposition, he has succeeded in getting us to do less and less strenuous work, under the pretext—true, but very difficult to get people to admit—that prolonged fatigue of the fingers is harmful to the quality of our performances. Moreover, during a performance of marches, in the middle of a snowstorm of exceptional vehemence, he persuaded Commander Schwarzhuber to let us return to our barracks. André has been careful not to argue that it is physically impossible for the musicians to continue playing in such inclement weather, but he has used arguments that are difficult to contradict, especially for a German who loves music: the instruments were in danger of deteriorating. And, little by little, the tradition has been established for us not to go out and play in bad weather. The SS had the opportunity to observe, not without astonishment, that the men were able to leave the camp without music, just as the corpses were able to return without ostentation!

All of these substantial changes have steadily contributed to the improvement of our mental and physical health by enabling us

## XI. MODULATIONS

to overcome the harshness of the Silesian winter. The first breath of spring of 1944 finds the music in a condition unknown until then.

Of course, we go out to work, as in the past, but our excursions now have the character of parties of pleasure rather than of imposed drudgery, and all musicians solicit these opportunities instead of seeking to avoid them.

More and more often, the itinerary of our trips leads us either to the Czech camp or to the women's camp, both of which are close to our own. Thus, our Doctor and his friend Michel have frequent opportunities to see their beloved relatives more closely. As for me, I cannot resist the somewhat sad attraction of these periodic visits. Like my comrades, I take advantage of the frequent slackening of surveillance to strike up a conversation with these beings, most of whom are devoid of their femininity. Little by little, charming friendships are created which are expressed by all the means at our disposal. We bring them food by taking from our rations or from our surplus. During the transportation of clothes and linen to the disinfection service one of us manages to steal women's clothes that we put under the car, in a good hiding place. We then take advantage of our next trip to the women's lodgings to give them the precious parcels in secret. Remembering the hard times of the past when I sought comfort from others, I now feel a real joy to be able, in my turn, to bring a little consolation to those who need it.

Our orchestra now numbers a little over forty men and our musical service is, more than ever, sanctioned by the German authorities. Apart from the two services intended for the departure and return of the commandos, we play, every Sunday afternoon, in public concerts. These are intended, in principle, for the SS, but the prisoners grouped around our stage also benefit from them. We now rehearse up to three times a week, and Franz Danisch, despite his frequent bullying, can be considered to support our cause.

Apart from the musicians, three other commandos are housed in our barracks. These are the electricians, the firemen and the construction workers. This last commando is one of the most important in the camp. It is employed in the preparation of materials for the construction of the barracks. Thanks to a friendly arrangement with one of the Kapos, André has obtained, with Danisch's consent, the enlargement and embellishment of the room reserved for our musical instruments. After two weeks of hard work, we now have a large and attractive room, with special facilities for instruments and for writing, and a comfortable arrangement for the clockmaker. In this room, a dozen or so musicians and their pupils can be accommodated. When circumstances permit, chamber music sessions are held here in the evening, in the presence of a select audience.

Little by little, I am beginning to forget that there was a time when I lived as a free man. It seems to me now that I have always lived this way and I feel less and less afraid that I will continue to live this way, between music and the carriage, for the rest of my life. The time of rebellion is over, I am perfectly reconciled with this reality that has become familiar to me. But will it always be like this?

No, because another reality, full of horror, looms before us.

Endless columns of men, women and children march past before our eyes dilated with horror. Coming from the train station and heading towards the gas chambers, they do not know where they are going. But the rest of us know that they are going to take part in a diabolical performance, carefully studied and designed to make them enter their graves. With a heart full of pain and pity for those who unknowingly go to their deaths, we are anxious about our own future.

## XI. MODULATIONS

Alongside these gloomy spectacles, we periodically experience tremors inside the camp that bring us back to this reality that we try in vain to ignore.

The selections! Every two or three weeks, a medical check-up takes place, carried out by the authorities. The weak, the sick, the mangy, all those who can no longer make a useful effort for the Germans and who are disdainfully called "Muslims" are inexorably isolated from the healthy and, after two or three days of waiting, sent in trucks to the crematorium. The music undergoes the same implacable sorting and even if, generally, we look good enough, our number is still reduced from time to time by one or two units. We all feel threatened by these selections, for the notion of "Muslim" is extremely flexible and the irrevocable death sentence depends only on the whim of the SS doctor who controls us. But the most unfortunate among us is the accordionist Bronek, with his stiff leg. At every selection we resort to very dangerous tricks to prevent him from showing up.

After each selection, the camp breathes a deep sigh of relief. The cloud has passed and we are back to good weather.

Our beautiful music room has become a place of pilgrimage for the SS and the camp's top leaders. Our barracks resounds with joyful tunes almost every evening. We sing, we dance. Birthdays are celebrated in style, and the SS attend, drinking brandy offered to them by the inmates.

Outside, there's the smoke of the crematorium during the day and the redness of the sky at night. And, jointly, we resume every day our customary work regarding the music and the manual labor with the car.

We visit the Czech camp several times to look for soap. Except for the barracks, the camp's existence is not at all like that of other camps. It is populated by Jews who live there in families. They keep their hair, their personal clothing, and receive letters and packages. In addition, they do not work. Their privileged treatment is an enigma for us and never ceases to arouse our envy.

They also have an ensemble of about fifteen musicians, some of whom sometimes come to our camp to copy the music they need.

Then, one day, bang! A painful surprise hits us like lightning in a clear sky.

For some time now, we have been short of music stands because the winter weather has damaged them and made them almost unusable. We have been trying to repair them on our own, by gluing and re-fixing them. Unfortunately, the wood is rotten from the moisture that has penetrated it, so our efforts are in vain. The foreman of the carpenters' commando promises to make us a few of them but, despite his promise, the delivery is delayed.

In the meantime, André is summoned to the commandant, Schwarzhuber, with some men. I go with him, intrigued by this summons.

The commandant tells us that he knew the band was short of music stands. He thought he would provide them, and he points to a dozen or so music stands in a corner, gesturing for us to take them away.

We recognize these objects. They come from the Czech camp and confirm the atrocious news that has spread since the day before: the four thousand Czechs were exterminated by gas, in one night, after six months of a comfortable life of which we were jealous!

Along with the music stands, we inherited from our Czech friends some violins, a saxophone, a trumpet and a cello. Our music is thus enriched. Its sound is more brilliant than ever.

André works as before, with obstinacy and indifference. I keep wondering how he reacts internally to everything that is happening around us. However, while I believe I have the right to question him,

## XI. MODULATIONS

now that he is my friend, I am always reluctant to get to the bottom of the problem, feeling confusedly that this would be dangerous ground to tread on.

One evening, however, I am rewarded for my long patience. For no apparent reason, I am given the opportunity to witness, alone, André's intimate outpourings and to gather a series of testimonies that allow me to judge more fully certain aspects of the world in which we move.

I will never forget the night we spent almost entirely chatting about the things that preoccupied me.

We had just given a very successful concert, at the end of which we had received great acclaim. Before going to bed, I wanted to congratulate André on his personal success and especially on the great advantages he had obtained for his musicians.

I found him alone in the room, dissimulating something under the table. Thinking I was disturbing him, I wanted to withdraw, but he invited me to sit down and removed the object from under the table. It was a bottle. Brandy!

I was stunned. I knew André had plenty of supplies, but I had heard that alcohol was strictly forbidden.

"Would you like some?" he asked.

I refused, without knowing why. André seemed to have had a few drinks already, judging by his glazed look.

"You're right, you don't eat well enough to drink brandy. But yes, I still have some. Every self-respecting prisoner has some. Every once in a while, it's good for you."

We sit down in a secluded corner of the room. André serves me bread, butter and salt. He only drinks from a cup, replacing the bottle under the table each time.

I feel at once that I will not have to question him and that he will speak for himself. Everything has come together for this: the sleeping barracks, the late hour, the drink. We both know that the moment of this confidential outpouring can no longer be postponed.

"Well," he begins, "I have the impression that you have been asking yourself too many things for a while… I suddenly feel like telling you my story, so here we are… It might amuse you…"

And this is what he tells me.

# XII. THEME AND VARIATIONS

"First, I have to describe to you," André begins, "what a normal day of 'work' outside was like in July of '42.

"Most of the commandos were extermination commandos where the question of more or less hard work did not even arise. The one I was part of went out every day with a strength of six hundred, only half of whom returned to the camp in the evening on their own two legs. We were surrounded by about fifty SS men, all young and handsome, bareheaded, with the sleeves of their green shirts rolled up to their elbows and holding legendary guard dogs on a leash. We were followed by a small truck to a construction site located about two kilometers away, to begin our day. It lasted from 6 a.m. to noon and from 12:30 to 6 p.m. The work itself was nothing extraordinary. You've done it many times before. It consisted of loading a sort of wheelbarrow with earth using two pairs of short sleeve shirts. It was carried by two people and was emptied a hundred meters away. When you had done this little job at a normal pace all day, you were simply exhausted, your legs refused to carry you, and you thought that if you had to do it again, you wouldn't last three days.

"Now imagine, if you can, that we had to run all day long under an uninterrupted hail of blows. The route we took was through a gauntlet of SS men who hit us with sticks or rifle butts to make us run faster and faster. Every hour, the Kapos picked up the corpses to load them onto the truck. The next day, six hundred of us went out again.

"Unbelievable as it may seem, after twenty days of this 'work' I was still alive.

"One night I learned that fifteen musicians had just arrived from Auschwitz I to form the core of an orchestra. More were to be hired. How could I introduce myself? I was stuck in either the commando or the block. I would get out of the clutches of one and fall under the thumb of the other. When we returned to our doghouses after a three-hour roll call, which you were lucky enough not to know, we were hungry with black lips parched with thirst and our bodies were swollen and flayed. Our feet were eaten up by lice and we couldn't take care of ourselves for a minute, so much so that we had to wait our turn to go to the latrines, collectively and under surveillance. There was no water in the camp. There was only one pump that worked exclusively for the kitchen. To get a drop, you had to pay for it with bread.

"It was under an unexpected circumstance that the opportunity presented itself to me to show my talents as a musician.

"One evening, we had just been given our rations and thrown into the kennels where we were squatting. I was nibbling a piece of bread when I heard our barracks leader, a murderer like all his colleagues, call out, 'Is there anyone among you who can play bridge?'

"I had already reached the point where one is no longer surprised by anything and, leaning out, I shouted with all my remaining strength: 'Me!'

"A few moments later, you could have seen me, dirty, repulsive, with a beard several days old, sitting comfortably with three eminences of the barracks, playing bridge in a small room, from which the groans of the massacred could be heard.

"These gentlemen were in the habit of playing this game quite regularly. But, that evening, the fourth partner was not available and my barracks' leader, saturated by his usual work—the murder of a few dozen men in order to get their rations—was absolutely determined to relax. That's why he had organized this bridge game, at the risk of involving, perhaps, one of his next victims, me in this case.

"It was during this game that I had the opportunity to tell him that I was a musician. He bitterly reproached me for not telling him earlier and took it upon himself to introduce me the next day.

## XII. THEME AND VARIATIONS

"In fact, he did much more than he had promised. When the game was over, he shaved me himself, cut my hair, lent me what I needed to wash myself, that is, a bowl of hot tea—not to drink, but to wash myself—soap and a towel, objects of the highest luxury. He also made sure that I did not go out with the commandos, gave me the remains of his personal meal and took me the next day to the musicians' barracks, where I was admitted immediately.

"During this period, the number of musicians changed almost every day. When I joined the orchestra, we were twenty. The day after, twenty-five. The next day, the number was reduced to twenty-one. A graph that would have recorded the variations in the number of members would have taken the form of a saw blade with some teeth missing. Our commando was, in this respect, similar to all the others.

"You told me recently that, on the night of your arrival, you heard some rifle shots that made a strong impression on you. These shots were fired by the SS sentries at those who approached the barbed wire with the intention of committing suicide. In 1942, the rifles were fired continuously throughout the night, because hundreds of unfortunate people who had had enough resorted to this simple way of ending their lives. And among them were musicians, members of the *Lagerkapelle*.

"The core of our band, as I said earlier, was made up of about fifteen former prisoners, sent from Auschwitz I where a large orchestra had existed for a long time. They had numbers between 2,000 and 16,000—I was, with my 49,000, a 'millionaire' at the time—and so they were the absolute masters of us, the new ones. Most of them used this power to the extreme and without limit. They could beat us, torment us, kill us, without accounting to anyone. Those of us who could no longer stand this treatment threw themselves against the electrified wires. These suicides only increased the frustration of our superiors. One day, when the number of musicians who had committed suicide the day before had been higher than usual, one of these gentlemen gathered those of us who were still alive and said the following: 'Sons of whores, I warn you that if you continue to go to the barbed wire, I will kill you all like dogs!'

"My knowledge of foreign languages had earned me a special privilege. Just after my accession to the orchestra, I was appointed almost official interpreter of the group. I was in charge of notifying the new members of the orders issued by our bosses. And I was, in accordance with the rules of this camp, held responsible for the execution of these orders, the slightest failure having to result in a corporal punishment that I alone suffered in place of the offenders.

"My admission to the orchestra had one advantage which I greatly appreciated: instead of being housed in a doghouse, I now had a proper bunk at my disposal. However, this success implied a duty which was for me an eternal nightmare. As soon as I got up, I had to make my bed, arranging the blankets in a certain way that was absolutely impeccable according to the instructions of the authorities. At any time of the day, an inspection could take place. And it was very difficult to get the blankets to fold to the desired shape to satisfy our inspectors! How often I had to sleep on the floor in a corner for fear of destroying a successful arrangement of my blankets, laboriously constructed in the morning!

"Shortly after my admission, I was afflicted with an intense fever, the cause of which I never knew and from which I could not get rid of until after two weeks. I continued to work anyway, sleeping standing up during work, sleeping sitting down during the music service, but not being able to sleep lying down at night. The hospital? You could go in as you pleased, you never left.

## XII. THEME AND VARIATIONS

"I have often wondered how much pain a human being can bear, what is the limit of their endurance, what is the point at which suffering makes them lose their animal attachment to life, however miserable and vile it may be. I have long sought the origin of this mysterious force which makes us endure a whole edifice of miseries, a tiny fraction of which would seem 'unbearable' under other conditions. I don't claim to have found the real psychological solution, but I think I can explain to you what happened to me.

"At that time, I was undergoing the effects of a multitude of exterminating elements, whereas only one of these elements should have been enough to annihilate me. The hunger, the thirst, the slave labor, the beatings, the illnesses, the roll calls, the groans of the tortured, the perpetual carnage, the lice, the corpses littering the camp—you didn't need all that to want to leave. It was truly 'unbearable' in the physiological sense of the word. And yet I put up with it, as did many others.

"For my part, I had made a firm resolution not to die voluntarily, no matter what. I wanted to see everything, to experience everything, to learn everything, to record everything. For what purpose? Since I would never have the opportunity to tell the world the result of my discoveries. Simply because I did not want to count myself out, to eliminate the witness that I could be.

"I was spared. The fever left me without reason, just as it had come, without my having taken a single pill or absorbed any medicine, that only a few chosen people possessed.

"And one day my life changed significantly.

"I had made a friend among the 'elders.' He was a man named Żuk, who had been arrested for teaching Polish illegally. He was gentle, a good comrade and never used the privilege of his seniority. Unlike most of his colleagues, he was human, simply human. He died a few weeks after having done me a service, insignificant in itself, but to which I may owe the pleasure of speaking to you at this moment.[7]

"One morning, when I was with other comrades near the truck loaded with coal that we had to take outside, Żuk came to inform me that I would be staying in the barracks all day to do some orchestrations. He had spoken about me to our music director at the time, a man named Zaborski, a Pole like himself, and obtained for me the unprecedented privilege of being part of the *Notenschreiber* (copyists) team. Franz Kopka was, at that time, the head of the barracks we occupied. He had been given this position because of his supposedly German nationality. Of course, he was always on our backs, giving us all kinds of improbable orders and poisoning our lives, which were difficult enough as it was. He was the drummer in the orchestra and therefore thought he was the mainstay of our music.

"Shortly after I took over as orchestrator, Zaborski fell ill and died in the hospital. He was a fairly erudite musician, less mean than the others, and he had enjoyed a certain authority among his subordinates. His death created an atmosphere of uncertainty in the music community, where no one was especially qualified to replace him. Kopka did not fail to take advantage of this confusion to obtain from the Germans his appointment to the post of conductor, to the great dismay of all the musicians, old and new. As for me, I felt a very legitimate terror. I was sure that the first act of the new leader would be to send me back to my old commando. We could not get along and Kopka had taken my enrollment into the writing office rather badly.

"However, it was the opposite that happened."

---

7. In fact, Żuk had not died. Laks relates how he learned about this in 1974 in *AM*, p.12. The correspondence that Laks and Żuk entertained between 1974 and Laks' death in 1983 is conserved in the Polish Library in Paris. [Ed. note]

# XIII. SUITE

"Placed in charge of an orchestra that now numbered about thirty men, Kopka soon realized his own professional inadequacy. The task before him was far too onerous, and the advantage he could gain from my presence in the music was not to be missed.

"Our repertoire was very modest at the time, and since the Germans demanded that we renew our programs as often as possible, and were very unhappy when we repeated the same marches, we had to increase our repertoire by all means. From time to time, we received piano scores or simply the vocal lines of marches that the SS brought back from Auschwitz I, but this was far from satisfying our needs. At the same time, we had to compose new marches in the German style or reconstruct the most well-known ones from memory, and then quickly orchestrate them. Fortunately, I was the only one capable of doing this, and Kopka knew it. Thus we were led to conclude, despite our mutual hatred, a sort of tacit pact. We both benefited from this: he by reaping all the official honors resulting from my work, and I by no longer being obliged, with very few exceptions, to go out to work.

"In my first orchestrations, I simply applied the knowledge I had acquired at liberty. In other words, I conformed strictly to the actual number of musicians at the time. But the constant fluctuations of our ensemble soon made this rigid method impractical.

"Time and time again, the sudden death of one or more performers left us with gaps of varying size, affecting the volume of sound in the ensemble. These gaps surprised me at first and led me to adopt, on a fairly large scale, the 'last resort' system of orchestration.

"You know that this system allows the performance of a piece with a greater or lesser number of musicians, without taking into account any gaps. The most important solos and motives are written in small print on the scores of each musician, which makes it possible to replace a missing instrument with another present.

"The adoption of this method of orchestration by 'arrangement' imposed upon me the sinister task of keeping a close watch on the physical and moral condition of my colleagues and of seeing to it that the 'last resorts' were applied to those of them who weren't about to be transferred to the hospital or to die or to commit suicide.

"In time, I became an expert in this funeral art, and the gaps disappeared in the sound of our orchestra. It was to be many months before the composition of the *Lagerkapelle* had stabilized and I was able to give up the role of musical mortician."

"Although our relationship was more or less settled, my collaboration with Kopka was full of unpleasant surprises, both for him and for myself. Because of his ignorance, he was unable to defend himself adequately against certain reproaches made by the Germans, some of whom were not without a certain musical education, and he was subjected to corporal punishment, sometimes quite serious. Not wanting to hide behind my person and thus disown his own, he meekly accepted the corrections, returning them to me afterwards with a generous interest. I remember a particularly characteristic and rather amusing episode, which will give you an idea of what this collaboration with Kopka was like, and which was to end only with his death.

"We had just received a new march from a famous German operetta that the SS absolutely wanted us to play. The orchestration had to be ready as soon as possible.

"At that time, the famous *Sonderkommando* (Special Commando) whose job, as you know, is to burn the corpses of the gassed, and who now lives next to the 'Crematorium,' still lived in our camp and went to work, like all the other commandos, to the sound of our music. The crematoriums were not yet built and the corpses were burned in ditches specially dug for this purpose. The *Sonderkommando* men were handling the often very decomposing dead bodies, and as they passed by, they gave off such a stench that one had to plug one's nose to avoid nausea.

"As luck would have it, the march in question took place at the same time as the Special Commando was marching past us. A pestilential wave bothered us. Suddenly, a young inmate who was acting as a 'messenger' for the SS ran up to us and ordered Kopka to change the music immediately and to report to the authorities after the service.

"I knew at once the reason for this order. The title of the march we had just interrupted was 'Berliner Luft,' that is, 'Berlin Air!'

"When we had finished playing, Kopka ran to the SS barracks. He returned after fifteen minutes, pale, unsteady on his feet and holding his buttocks with his hands. He had just received twenty-five blows there. The Germans did not believe it was a coincidence and accused him of having premeditated this inappropriate mockery.

"As soon as he returned, without telling me anything, Kopka, as I had expected, gave me the same number of blows.

"From that day on, we were careful not to play 'Berlin Air' until the Special Command had already gone outside.

"The improvement in my condition came when we moved from the old camp to this one and Kopka was replaced as barracks leader by the famous Albert Haemmerle.[8]

---

8. Born on October 13, 1920 in Tübingen, green triangle, common law, deported to Auschwitz from Dachau on May 8, 1941. [Ed. note]

"Haemmerle was one of the oldest prisoners in the camp. He had been part of the team of German Kapos that the SS had brought from other camps to educate the first deportees from Poland. He was a common law prisoner who wore a green triangle and had a reputation for not sitting down to breakfast until he had knocked out forty prisoners in his block. Albert Haemmerle was of average height, rather frail, and at first glance there was no evidence of his extraordinary physical strength. He was a real champion in the field of wrestling outside your weight class. I once saw him knock down his colleague, a giant armed with a club, who, after a few minutes of fighting, had been brought down by Albert's fists alone.

"As soon as we moved into the new barracks, we could see with our own eyes the havoc Albert wreaked on the ranks of his boarders, either during roll call or at night. His victims numbered in the thousands and, by dint of his relentless attacks, in his barracks and even in those of others, he ended up alarming his colleagues, who made him understand that he was too zealous in his task and that this risked harming them with the Germans. But Albert continued to do so, until the authorities interfered, notifying him that each case of death he caused would henceforth be the subject of a detailed report on its causes.

"Yet this dangerous roommate, who unleashed against all, was the friend of our orchestra, and mine especially. Without mercy for the slightest offense on the part of others, he tolerated almost every license of the musicians, provided they did not get caught by the Germans. His friendship for me had a special origin.

"Albert's secretary was a young, handsome man named Jean, a Polish national. A tender love seemed to unite the two men. Jean was my first English student. This relationship benefited me doubly. I was paid in bread, sausage, margarine and soup supplements. Moreover, these lessons earned me a certain reputation in the barracks, and, above

## XIII. SUITE

all, a kind of protection from Haemmerle, which had the immediate result of increasing Kopka's regard for me.

"One day Jean left his lover to go to another among the privileged ones. I never knew whether it was a matter of sentiment or of interest. Albert, like a wounded beast, unleashed his fury on his subordinates, and the number of dead bodies littering his barracks became higher than ever.

"Our orchestra, however, did not suffer. On the contrary: during the long weeks following Jean's departure, he had tender romances performed in the evenings, trying to escape his boredom. When the musical sessions were over, he invited me to his room and made me write passionate love letters to the one who had abandoned him. Each time, I would come back with a lot of food.

"And that's how I was able to survive…"

André's bottle is empty now. He is half-drunk himself, but I am impressed by his lucidity. I ruminate on my thoughts and get ready to return to bed, but he holds me back.

"Listen, I didn't tell you all this to describe my personal misfortunes. It doesn't matter. There are others who have probably suffered more than I have. I wanted you to compare the old life in the camp with the present one. When I told you that we were now in a sanatorium, it was obviously just a manner of speaking. When I arrived here, I was told more or less the same thing. A little more, a little less, what does it matter? However, you must have noticed that the inmates are now living better and better, and that this improvement is correlated with the ever-increasing flow of those who, coming from outside, are directed to the crematorium without receiving any number. You will therefore understand how difficult it is for me to eat my fill, to quench my thirst, to be well dressed, to lead the life of a privileged person..."

I don't immediately understand the meaning of this remark and I don't know what to say. Something else worries me and I tell André about it.

"Yes," he replies, "I expected this question, everyone asks it. Do you want to know why the others go to the oven and not us? Well, it's quite simple, basically, although at first glance we don't understand anything. We, stranded here by the capricious will of a manpower recruitment officer, form the category of 'useful mouths' and the Germans believe they need us for the moment. We survived, some by luck, some by weakness of character, some by lack of scruples. We are the administrative staff of the camp, so to speak, making a number of Germans available for slightly more 'intimate' work. In many ways, we are all a small but concrete part of the formidable German war machine. Because the German cannot imagine anything without music, ours is also a substantial cog in this machine. The slightest movement of your shovel, even if you only pretend to move it, the slightest push of the car that makes it move, contributes, whether you like it or not, to the German war effort. On the other hand, we 'old-timers' are called upon to receive with dignity and to educate the generations of 'millionaires' who, in turn, will succumb to the privations of the beginning, leaving a few survivors adapted to the 'regime'...

"But how do you explain how one part of humanity could resolve to destroy another in cold blood? It seems to me so monstrous, so incompatible with... the universal conception of morality..."

"It's obvious, but someone had to think of it. And the German thought of it. It is enough to understand the principle. Have you ever felt remorse when you crushed a louse? To the Germans, we are all lice. We, I mean first of all the Jews, enemies of Germany by its very doctrine. Then it will be the turn of all the Russians, of all the Poles, and all the French, in short, of all those who, in the eyes of the Germans, are inassimilable to their conception of the race of the lords... Thus, within a hundred years, there will be only Germans in Europe. And in five hundred years, our planet will be populated only by Germans. It will finally be paradise!"

"Do you really believe that?"

"No," André replied, smiling, "of course not. It won't be... simply because the Germans will lose this war, just as they lost the one in 1914. But they started it assuming that victory was certain. That's why they didn't hesitate to start this activity of exterminating people. The completion of this immense task is only a question of time. The construction of the Auschwitz camp was planned to last fifteen years, three of which have already passed. At the moment, the entire facility can hold about 250,000 people. In 1956, this capacity should reach five million! A kind of flush for the waste of humanity, eh!

I cling to an idea.

"If you are convinced that the Germans will lose the war, we might have a chance to get out of it?" André looks at me curiously, then answers:

"But of course!" The tone of this reply, however, is far from reassuring.

# XIV. PRESTO CON FUOCO

Indeed, the German war machine seems to be working at maximum efficiency. I can no longer doubt that the gas chambers, like the crematoriums, are its main elements.

Around us, thousands of human beings, gathered from the four corners of Europe, are devoured daily by the insatiable Nazi Moloch. This holocaust has been going on for almost two years. It began timidly with the sacrifice of the exhausted and of those unable to make any effort, and gradually increased thanks to the incessant arrivals, so high in number that they could no longer be absorbed by the camp's labor needs. The Germans are in a hurry. In order to avoid having to walk part of the way, a special track has been built, by the prisoners of course, linking the arrival station to the facilities serving as an antechamber to the crematoriums.

This is how we can see in front of us, during the hours of our musical service, a real tower of Babel in motion: Russians, Poles, French, Dutch, Greeks, Lithuanians, quietly making their way to the places of their perdition, lulled by the music they hear from afar.

The climax of this grandiose action of annihilation seems to have been reached with the arrival of the Hungarians in dozens of trains a day. Each train contains two to three thousand martyrs. We, the former residents, are nevertheless aware of what is happening since the camp's abominations have become almost familiar sights for us. But every time we watch, powerless, these parades of convicts, we shudder with horror as at the first vision. Each time our brains burst, unable to conceive the juxtaposition of these two separate worlds, one of which, outside the camp, was created for a rapid and massive extermination, the other, inside, for a slower, more methodical, more economical, more profitable destruction.

Every day, a few survivors swell the ranks of the prisoners and

## XIV. PRESTO CON FUOCO

complete the number of workers reduced by the selections that occur about twice a month. We know by heart the traditional questions that the new tattooed prisoners ask us: "Where are we? What did they do with our luggage? When will we see our families?" Etc... We answer as we had been answered in the past, when we landed, stammering half-consolations and half-denials. Then, these "millionaires" infallibly give us news of the war. It's funny how optimistic they can be! They are all the same, all incorrigible. If you believe them, the Germans have already lost the war, they are retreating everywhere, they have almost no rolling stock left and we expect the Allies to land any moment now...

This refrain, which is sung to us at each new arrival and which, in similar circumstances, was once ours, leaves us cold. Don't the Germans have any more rolling stock? Come on! We shouldn't have to see all these innumerable trains of future corpses, brought back precisely from the places where they claim to have chased the Germans! And then, in the end, good or bad, how can this news concern us? It comes from a world that we have known, certainly, in the past, but which remains buried for us forever. Our universe, much more concrete, differs totally from this lost world, and the vague echoes that reach us from there can change nothing. Our life is our own. We live in music, we eat our fill, we enjoy the joys of love, in a word, our present life is probably more comfortable than that of many free people.

If the crematoriums are abundantly supplied with human flesh, our prison compound is increasingly provided with food and earthly goods of all kinds. If tens of thousands of human beings are burned every day, we are careful not to do the same with their luggage and belongings. On their way to death, each person leaves behind everything they brought with them. The arrival platform is littered with deformed mounds of suitcases, necessities, shopping bags, improvised packages. Waiting to be rifled through, all these disparate parcels form a heap sometimes reaching the height of a building: a real gigantic still life.

There is a commando assigned to the handling, classification and transportation of all these riches. It is officially called the Clearing Commando, but everyone, even the SS, calls it "Canada," a familiar name, a symbol of abundance. And, in fact, there is everything in "Canada."

This commando's strength was originally two hundred. It has just been increased to eight hundred or more. The work is very closely supervised, because most of the loot, except for perishable goods, is destined to be sent to the interior of the Reich, for "poor little Germans." However, it is tolerated that the "Canada workforce" take small quantities of food for their own use. This tolerance is extremely flexible, since the limited number of SS guards do not allow for perfect control.

The Canada workforce prisoners have a particularly skillful technique for concealing items taken from the Germans. Their pockets are quite deep and clever hiding places, made by a specialized tailor, allow them to store a large amount of loot. None of them is unaware that a check may be waiting for them when they return to the camp, but they also know that the SS do not have the material possibility to search everyone and that most of them manage to pass without leaving anything in the hands of the checkers. Then there is another way to preserve what has been stolen. It is enough to make a tightly tied bundle and to throw it over the barbed wire on the way back to the camp, which makes it possible to present oneself in good standing at the control, i.e. "nothing in the hands, nothing in the pockets." The accomplices, who are on the lookout for the return of the commando, take it upon themselves to hide the parcel until it is time to distribute it fairly among those concerned.

## XIV. PRESTO CON FUOCO

Precious stones, wedding rings, gold and paper dollars, watches, cigarettes, alcohol, perfume, fine linens, clothing, chocolate, hams, chickens, smoked bacon, canned goods, condensed milk and other choice items, all enter our prison in an uninterrupted stream, often thanks to the benevolent blindness of our guards.

All this is only the culmination of the small traffic that began long before the blossoming of the camp life, almost at the threshold of its history, with the first death.

As soon as a corpse had been "realized," the first instinctive move of its neighbor was to rob it. With a bit of luck, he could find on it a piece of bread, a piece of string, a penknife, a razor blade, a needle. The recovery of these objects already constituted a modest enrichment for the recipient, thanks to the possibility of exchange with his comrades. In the event of the death of a "wealthy" prisoner, the inheritance was more substantial: shoes, cigarettes, a watch, gold teeth, etc.

In Auschwitz, there was no shortage of dead people. The goods they were stripped of fed the market that was thus inaugurated.

In some privileged places, their attendants were able to take a considerable part of what they were handling and put it into the stream of "business." In the kitchen, in the canteen, in the clothing store, in the supply store and even in the hospital, meat, fat, vegetables, clothing, linen and medicine intended for the supply of the prisoners were removed from the official distributions and became private property.

All of this, added to the "merchandise" coming from the despoiling of hundreds of thousands of people sent directly to the gas chambers, ended up generating a prodigious economic world, with its privileged and proletarian classes, with its prices, with its fluctuations, with a stock market. A currency had been imposed for a long time and no one thought of challenging it. It was, for us, a golden value. Without it, no evaluation of an article was possible. This unit of currency was the cigarette.

Like inflation, the abundance of smokable material caused its value to fall. Its scarcity led us to resort to the fractioning of each unit. Butts also had their value. In "normal" times—that is to say, when the rate of arrival was regular—a loaf of bread was worth twelve cigarettes, a five-hundred-gram packet of margarine cost thirty, a watch between eighty and two hundred, and a liter of alcohol four hundred.

As an independent and respectable country, we also had our trade with foreign countries. Our clientele included a large number of civilian workers assigned as technicians to certain commandos, who were big consumers of linen, clothing and shoes that only the inmates of the Birkenau camp were able to provide. In the ranks of the commandos who went out to work in the morning, there were many who wore almost new civilian suits under their striped uniforms and who were superbly shod. In their pockets, more than one valuable piece of jewelry, more than one gold coin was carefully hidden. In the evening, they came back with old shoes or clogs and had only their regular clothes on their backs. But in return for what they had left outside, their pockets contained fine bottles of brandy, fresh butter, country cold cuts and German cigarettes of the best brands.

The whole of these operations, both internal and external, had an established name, adopted by all, prisoners and SS, although no one knew its origin. It was "the organization."

# XV. SYMPHONY OF CHAOS

To "organize" means to obtain anything by any of the following means: purchase, donation, exchange, begging or theft.

One "organizes" a piece of bread or ten loaves of bread, a rag or fine linen, a cigarette or a thousand cigarettes, a liter of soup or a barrel of soup, a plank or a shack! We "organize" a little salt, a bucket of coal, a truckload of firewood, medicine, a sweater, a straw mattress, a bunk, we "organize" everything! Our beautiful medical office had its expansion and embellishment "organized" from scratch, because although the Germans had authorized us to carry out the necessary work, they had not given us the means to do it. They told us to "organize it all." And it was the building commando—who lived in our hut—who provided us with the manpower and the material, and this in exchange for accordion lessons with the commando's foreman and the permission to practice in the enlarged room. Thus, our music has "organized" a nice room, luxuriously furnished, while the foreman is delighted to have "organized" his music lessons so cheaply. Another example: on the day we inherited our new music stands from the gassed Czech musicians, we were asked the traditional question: "How did you manage to 'organize' these beautiful music stands?"

After the evening roll call, most of the inmates are busy with the "organization" which often goes on beyond lights out. Everyone "organizes" what they can, and the whole camp is dotted with small groups of businessmen gesticulating wildly and scattering hastily at the sight of a German uniform.

But there is a spacious and safer place, reserved for meetings of traders of all kinds: thieves, fence-sitters, beggars, sellers and buyers. This place is the latrine. It is held in a shack, similar to all the others, but transformed into a toilet and able to accommodate six hundred clients simultaneously. This is where the big fair of the small-time dealers is held. One can exchange razor blades for a ration of sausage, sewing thread for a liter of soup from the previous day, a ration of moldy bread for a few cigarette butts, a spoon whose handle has been sharpened to serve as a knife for a piece of cheese, a little saccharine for a few raw or cooked potatoes. One can exchange anything for anything, calculating the value of the merchandise according to that of a cigarette. The latrine is the stock exchange of the proletariat, the court of miracles, the flea market of the camp. No self-respecting prisoner would come there for any other reason than physiological, unless it was for curiosity. Moreover, a small corner of the latrine is strictly reserved for the Kapos and other camp luminaries. A common prisoner could not go there without being beaten or thrown into the cesspool as a warning for the future.

An entirely different kind of stock exchange session is held in the private rooms of representatives of the possessing classes. The seclusion of these compartments allows the often delicate and risky transactions to take place in complete safety. Watches, jewelry, gold teeth, dollars, rings and pendants are exchanged for cigarettes by the hundreds, for food and delicacies, for labor and construction materials, and sometimes, with the complicity of the SS, for German military uniforms to facilitate a planned escape.

It is tacitly accepted that the Kapos and barracks leaders live, two or three to a room, very comfortably set up, with individual bunks equipped with clean sheets, cushions, blankets in sufficient quantities, with stoves on which they can cook.

These rooms are equipped with tiled windows, curtains, carpets and other items that seem to be of primary necessity to them. It is also a rule that each privileged person has a "*Kalifaktor*," a sort of servant, who is responsible for cleaning the room, cooking and any other services that his boss may need. The "*Kalifaktor*" is generally responsible for "organizing" the room for his master, negotiating what the latter entrusts to him on his return each evening and which he must give up at the most advantageous price.

Where did all this construction material come from, boards, walls, plywood, pillars, doors, glass, roofing, which were used to build these small private rooms, of which there are an average of four per hut? This material was not supplied by the Germans, for the simple reason that it was not included in the construction plan for the Auschwitz camp.

There are small "organizers," just as there are medium and large ones, depending on their degree of wealth. The "respectability" of a prisoner is measured by the extent of his means of "organization." We have a few chosen ones, whose situation allows them to "organize" on such a large scale that it is beyond any means of control on the part of the Germans, given the large number of the latter engaged in this type of operation. The most famous of all these "organizers" was undoubtedly Reinhold, the *Oberkapo*—Kapo principal—of the building's commando.

Interned for about ten years, Reinhold stayed in almost all German camps to finally end up in Auschwitz. He had a green triangle—it is said that he had been arrested for major tax evasion—and was recently exempted from wearing any triangle, as a reward for his "exceptional merits." In fact, he is the only prisoner who enjoys this privilege and everyone considers him an "honorary prisoner." He has also been granted the favor of growing his hair, a favor he cannot enjoy because he is completely bald.

The *Oberkapo* Reinhold's lifestyle is a burden to everyone. His breakfast consists of eggs and ham, washed down with a bowl of real coffee with real whole milk. It is said that his table is far superior to that of our commander. He has a small cellar, hidden under the floor of his room, with the best German and French wines, branded liquors and dozens of liters of pure alcohol. The SS consider it a great honor to be invited to his meals. Outside, at the construction site, where

Reinhold goes every day with his commando, a small barracks was set up for his personal use, equipped with all the comforts one could imagine in such a place.

The traffic that Reinhold deploys, because of his situation, could be the subject of a separate book.

He controls all of the construction material for the barracks placed at his disposal by the camp authorities, and uses it as he pleases, practically without having to account for it to anyone, even though he is officially required to provide a detailed report every three months on the consumption of materials and the work done.

Reinhold was at the head of a commando of 800 people, including half a dozen Kapos, his "grey eminences" as far as the "organization" was concerned, who were in charge of exchanging construction materials for choice foodstuffs or objects of value. Through them, Reinhold provides the privileged prisoners in all the camps around Auschwitz with the materials they need to build and furnish their private rooms.

In winter, during the fuel shortage, stools, tables and entire bunks disappear into the heating stoves.

But it is the Germans themselves who formed Reinhold's most numerous and most reliable clientele. About twenty specialized cabinetmakers work under Reinhold's direction to fulfill orders from SS officers, non-commissioned officers and soldiers. These orders are for luxury furniture for their homes near the camp. Carefully finished and varnished lounges, cabinets, bedrooms, children's carriages and sports equipment are regularly delivered to the Germans, to the detriment of the camp's barracks' layout.

For some time now, there has been talk of freeing Reinhold. At a reception organized—in both senses of the word—for this occasion, and after several rounds, Reinhold good-naturedly confessed in the presence of a few SS, his guests, to having squandered, during the last six months, the material for thirty-five barracks!

## XV. SYMPHONY OF CHAOS

We laughed heartily at this excellent story and, to glorify Reinhold's admirable feat, everyone drank to his health, to the health of the commandant and, finally, to that of the Führer.

# XVI. SERENADES

Music is a luxury item and, as such, an essentially "organizable" material. Musicians know this and take advantage of opportunities to negotiate their talents with those who can afford it. The leading figures of the camp whose position is firmly established, whose income is stable, and who have a virtually inexhaustible supply of food like to entertain themselves in privacy with the sounds of music.

It is customary for them to approach the *Kapellmeister* to obtain a "rental" of three or four musicians. This permission is, of course, subject to a fee and is part of the conductor's system of "organization." The pretext for these small, intimate sessions is provided, in most cases, by birthdays or prison anniversaries or name days of the Kapos or the assimilated, dates which the friends of the Kapos want to celebrate in style.

According to an established tradition, the ceremony takes place in two stages.

The first takes place at dawn, before the general awakening. The designated musicians get up well before everyone else, so that they are close to the person's bunk with their instruments, a few seconds before the gong—the wake-up call—sounds. They then start a triumphal march that pleasantly awakens the sleeper. The sleeper, touched by this delicate attention, supposedly unexpected, hastens to hand out gifts to the wake-up musicians. A few bars of a languid melody conclude this first part of the solemnity.

The second part usually takes place in the private room of the "leading figure," in the evening, after the roll call. The number of musicians is often greater and the concert more varied. The recipient and his friends gather around a well-stocked table and the meal is accompanied by a copious amount of alcohol. After the reception, everyone listens religiously to the tunes of their countries, sometimes

## XVI. SERENADES

evoking memories of their time in freedom. Sometimes an SS man appears during the party, but the party is not disturbed by this. On the contrary, his arrival adds to the exuberance of the gathering. Everyone is drinking and singing at the top of their voices and the party goes on late into the night.

But this is nothing compared to the celebration of *Oberkapo* Reinhold's birthday.

Although he had his own room, he made sure that the entire barracks was part of the celebration. In addition, almost all of the SS were present.

Reinhold was awakened first by an aubade-fanfare performed by the entire orchestra. He got out of bed in his silk pajamas, rubbed his eyes, and walked with a heavy step to his cupboard, taking out hundreds of cigarettes which he distributed generously to the musicians. Then, taking a few bottles of liquor, he made us drink one after the other, shaking hands cordially with each of us. We thanked him by playing a second piece, while people from all sides crowded around to congratulate him. And when, half an hour later, Reinhold, handsome as a prince, marched at the head of his building commando to his work and "organization" site, we interrupted the march in progress to play his favorite tune.

In the evening, a monstrous banquet took place in our barracks, followed by a night ball, and the chicest districts in the most cosmopolitan cities had nothing on our banquets.

While these charming parties are taking place periodically inside the camp, the terrible rhythm of the arrivals of human fuel remains steady outside.

The number of "special commandos" turns out to be insufficient and they are reinforced every day with men who have been lucky enough to escape the gas. Instead of being burned, they will burn the others.

Nor is the Canada able to provide the clearing service on its own. After having increased the number of men by drawing on the ranks of various commandos who are less overworked, we musicians are finally called upon to help out the Canada section.

The thirty musicians assigned to this task are delighted with their lot. To be employed as a Canada worker is a real boon, because nowhere is there so much "organization."

There is not a shadow of remorse in us, not the slightest scruple haunting us. Since we cannot stop this deluge of corpses, why not take advantage of the days that are offered to us and which are perhaps the last of our life here below?

Joyfully, we rush towards the ramp, our new construction site.

At first, we are disappointed. The first job we have to do is the most unpleasant of all and the goods we handle are practically "unorganizable."

In the recently arrived train, emptied of its occupants and their luggage, all that remains in each car is a large container that has served the natural needs of the passengers. These containers are full to the brim and we have to empty them into a car equipped for this purpose. In principle, there is a commando assigned to this kind of chore, but we learn that it is busy repairing the blocked sewers somewhere in the vicinity. The filled car is driven by us to a large excavation located two hundred meters from the ramp. It must be unloaded there. A real battle ensues between all of us during this operation, which everyone would like to avoid at all costs. The car is emptied with the help of a large drain plug, the removal of which has the effect of splashing the person handling it. In the evening, after several trips of this kind, we are impregnated with a foul odor that we can hardly get rid of, although we change clothes before our performance.

## XVI. SERENADES

Fortunately, our despair does not last long. The sewage commando has finished its work of unblocking and claims its usual job. We are freed from our slurry tank and assigned to tasks more similar to what is usually done in the "Canada" section.

This is not without its pitfalls. The "Canada" workers do not look kindly on our competition with them. They try to relegate us to the back seat by making us clean the cars which, although empty of baggage, are full of dirt and detritus of all kinds. These had to be loaded onto a small car and taken back to the camp. This is no different than our previous occupation and we are all in a very bad mood.

But luck favors us. The pace of the convoys being dumped on the docks is such that we barely have enough time to clean the empty train before it has to make way for a new train full of men. Thanks to the disarray caused by the tumultuous descent of the deportees, we can finally get our hands on the parcels and quickly examine their contents. Each of us manages to get hold of a precious package which, unnoticed by the SS and the Canada workers, we hide in the garbage that our car had been loaded with. Sure of not being searched by the Germans, we bring our booty home.

Our collaboration with the Canada workers, which was rich in "organizational" means, and which lasted several weeks, was followed by a few visits to the *Effektenlager* or Personal Effects Camp. This is nothing more than a huge warehouse where, after sorting, all the luggage and effects belonging to the deportees and destined to be sent to Germany are stored.

When you enter this barbed-wire enclosure, you can see a double row of barracks identical to ours, but the difference is that these barracks contain no inmates, only objects. Each barracks is marked with an inscription indicating the item stored. Thus, there is the laundry barracks, the shoe barracks, the blanket barracks, etc... In one corner of the camp, we can see a pile of various objects that seem to be destined for the waste. Among these miscellaneous objects, one can distinguish: glasses, prayer books, children's dolls, photographs, passports, walking sticks, umbrellas…

The *Effektenlager* is served by a large number of specialized personnel, recruited from among the prisoners, of course, to whom the sorting, classification and custody of all the objects are entrusted. They never leave the premises. Most of these staff are young, pretty women, elegantly dressed—not in striped clothes—and one would be tempted to think that they are ladies of high society, in a big city, in peacetime. The only difference is that they have, like all the prisoners, the serial number sewn prominently on their chests.

Clearly, everything they wear and everything they eat comes from an obvious "organization." Having the custody of several dozen buildings bursting with wealth, assisting in the sorting of millions of small objects of daily use, how is it surprising that these women differ so much from their sisters who live a few hundred meters away, in the deepest misery? The lovely creatures we are now contemplating live in small barracks with curtained windows and furnished with the maximum of comfort. They sleep in individual beds, with regularly changed sheets and thick, nicely arranged blankets. They have make-up, perfume, cologne, silk stockings. Their hairstyles seem to come from the caressing hands of the best hairdressers in Paris. Except for freedom, they have everything a woman can dream of. They even knew about love, which the proximity of the men, prisoners and SS, made inevitable.

When we leave the *Effektenlager* and its anonymous riches, we think we are leaving a land of dreams.

But the enchantment dissipates immediately. Ten meters away, on the other side of the barbed-wire fence, stand the rectangular chimneys of the crematoriums that burn, burn without ceasing, the owners of the luggage that the lovely creatures we have just left are handling.

# XVII. DIRECTED CACOPHONY

I must do justice to the Germans. Contrary to the opinion that may have been formed from various hearsay, it is not entirely true that the music we were making there was intended to officially accompany the manifestations of horror, such as the transport of victims to the gas chambers, shootings, hangings, public canings, etc... There were, of course, so many instances of such scenes occurring simultaneously with our musical performances that one was supposed to consider these coincidences as intentional. In reality, this was the effect of chance and of a lack of administrative correlation of these two branches of activity, as was the case everywhere else.

In order to understand the Machiavellian institution of the German extermination camp, you have to convince yourself that the most characteristic element is the absence of any contact between the countless services of the camp. The state of mind that was formed had been thoroughly studied by specialists and the most essential basis of these studies was the perfect knowledge of man's weaknesses, of his vilest inclinations, of the sovereignty of his instinct for self-preservation, and of his innate disposition for any crime, provided that it remained unpunished.

The carefree life led by the privileged prisoners, the contempt of the strong for the weak, the indifference with which the healthy considered a dying man, the market that flourished in the camp, the thoughtless joy with which the "organizers" welcomed the transports of men who were going to their deaths, leaving behind "good merchandise," all of this proved the accuracy of the psychological calculations of the German scientists.

It was materially impossible for a prisoner of "good will" to comply with all the camp's instructions. Anyone who wanted to be an exemplary prisoner would have been like a man who decided to take advantage of all the praise on the billboards of a large city and to buy all the items advertised there.

The orders came from several centers, each of which had countless independent sectors. Orders poured in from all sides, simultaneously, counteracting or contradicting each other. They each had a different origin, a different purpose and seemed to result from individual considerations not coordinated with the general line of the German plan. There were orders of a political, sanitary, food, numerical, economic, clothing, moral and aesthetic character. The services overlapped one another and the executors often did not know what to do. One was tempted to believe that the Germans did not know how to carry out the formidable task they had undertaken. However, one only had to look at the fruits of their "inability" to realize how much of this chaos was intended, premeditated, and expected, not only for the present but for centuries to come.

Let's take a look at all the services that operated within our prison.

The entire camp was dotted with moral inscriptions, each more exemplarily than the next. At the entrance, it read: "Work is freedom." In every corner of the barracks, this maxim: "There is only one road that leads to freedom. The milestones that mark it are honesty, diligence, cleanliness, work, obedience and respect for one's superiors."

On the other hand, in order to try to survive the camp atmosphere, the inmate was forced to resort to continuous immorality and his only concern was, as we have seen above, not to let himself be caught red-handed. If he was still alive a few days after his landing, he had already understood all the shameless cynicism of the commands we have just mentioned.

The prisoner was required to make a maximum physical effort to contribute to the functioning of the German war machine.

On the other hand, the circumstances that conditioned his work

## XVII. DIRECTED CACOPHONY

were such that he was unfit, after a few days, for any real effort. He was therefore suppressed, either by beatings or by selections. He could only survive by evading the vigilance of his executioners, that is, by pretending to work and by "organizing."

We had a quasi-modern hospital, with qualified personnel, with numerous therapeutic facilities and with extra rations of food provided for the sick, such as white bread, semolina, sugar, pasta, etc.

On the other hand, even if some were lucky enough to recover and join the ranks of the healthy, an administrative routine resulted in the periodic emptying of the hospital of its sick, directing them to the crematorium, often at the very moment they were cured.

The camp received quantities of food sufficient, in theory, to feed all the prisoners. Official reports on the collection and distribution of food were provided daily to the German supply center. These reports specified, among other things, the quantities of choice products allocated to children, the weak, the sick, the elderly and pregnant women.

On the other hand, the SS tolerated, encouraged and took personal advantage of the regular squandering of food intended for distribution. The rations were constantly reduced, the nutritious products intended for the kitchen were diverted by the manipulators and thrown into the "organization" market. The prisoner was given a soup devoid of fat, meat and potatoes, which were replaced by nettles and apple or cabbage peelings. But the camp authorities were able, at any time, to provide material proof that each prisoner remained as well fed as the German soldier at the front.

There was only one exception to this scheme of things, and it was the one around which all the anomalies listed above revolved. It was the accuracy of the daily verification of the number of prisoners. It had to correspond, to the nearest man, alive or dead, to the figure in the file service. We were at our wits' end if a missing person was reported. We remained at the call, during all kinds of bad weather, until he was found. And watch out for him: he never came out alive.

The effects of the frequent clashes between the official view and reality contributed to the maintenance of chaos. Our musical performances only increased it. At the same time as we were torn apart by an inner revolt, we carelessly accepted to take part in it, to the great satisfaction of our audience and the performers.

But the images of the camp scenes in which the music took part are not about to fade from my memory.

On this day, a day like so many others, the four crematoriums are burning at full capacity. They can no longer suffice. We uncover and widen the old ditches that were used before the crematoriums were built. A permanent, acrid, black cloud of burnt grease hovers in the sky and over our heads, seeming to want to take us with it.

This day is a day like many others, but not for everyone. It is the birthday of our commander, SS *Hauptsturmführer* Schwarzhuber. The SS pack is reveling in the fuss of great events. Franz Danisch is in a state of excitement and for the first time takes us seriously. He has allowed us to rehearse for several days the big concert we are to give on the occasion of this festival. He has ordered us to greet the arrival of the *Lagerführer* with a specially written fanfare of trumpets, and long before the appointed time he has instructed us to set up with our instruments.

In our familiar place, we wait for the visit of our chief executioner, while playing a piece. From our vantage point, we can contemplate, once again, the long line of condemned people who pass by, some on foot, others in trucks, and who, attracted by the sounds of the music, turn their heads our way.

## XVII. DIRECTED CACOPHONY

Franz Danisch keeps running to the front door to watch for the commander's car. Not long afterwards, he signals us to stop and prepare to greet the hero of the day.

The moving crowd of the sacrificed comes to a standstill. The commander's car appears and stops in front of the entrance. All is silence. Only the cloud of smoke stirs in the sky. The car door opens and the elegant figure of Schwarzhuber, in his new uniform and cap, emerges from the doorway.

The jubilant fanfare of our trumpets rips through the silence. The *Lagerführer* stands at attention, pressing the palm of his right hand against the visor of his hat. Danisch, stiffened, bareheaded, his chest bulging, stands nearby, ready to run at the slightest gesture of the commander. The members of the SS staff, frozen and servile, are all present.

As soon as the trumpets fall silent, we begin the first number of our program. In the meantime, other people have stepped out of the car: a woman and two children, aged six to eight. Between them, they make up the Schwarzhuber family. The wife is ravishingly fresh, healthy, and beautiful, and she holds her husband lovingly by the arm. The two blond children, like two legendary cherubs, surround the happy couple. The commander speaks to his people, pointing to our camp. He probably has to explain to them how the evil enemies of the beloved Führer are punished and chastised. However, he must not tell them where the smoke that blackens the sky is coming from. Nor does he tell them that at this time of day, SS *Oberscharführer* Mohl, who is in charge of the crematorium, is having fun with other small children, taking them by the legs to smash their little heads against a wall, and also practicing shooting at the young mothers, aiming at their lower stomachs and then, when they have fallen, at the tips of their breasts.

*Lagerführer* Schwarzhuber orders us to play *"Heimat deine Sterne."*

Why don't we, instead of carrying out his order, grab his two beautiful children and throw them into the flames and make the parents suffer the anguish that so many others are experiencing!

It is still a day like so many others! But not for the three Russians who escaped the day before and who had the misfortune to be recaptured.

The commandos have just returned to the camp. For the first time, we do not have to leave our platform to go to roll call. We pass the checkpoint from where we are standing. All the men are gathered in front of their barracks. A gloomy tension reigns everywhere.

Three gallows stand about ten feet in front from us. It is not unusual to see escapees hanged, but today the ceremony is a little different. The cannon has been sounding for some time, probably to remind us that we are not abandoned, that the Russian troops are advancing and that there is fighting less than a hundred kilometers away.

All the SS men enter the camp. Without distinction of rank, they are armed with automatic weapons. All the camp's inhabitants are also gathered at the execution site. The three condemned men are then brought in, their hands tied behind their backs. The SS's anxiety rises at the same time as our anger. They point their machine guns nervously in the air, while other machine gunners in the watchtowers surrounding the camp point their guns at us. The three Russians are perched on tables placed under each rope. An agonizing silence follows the murmurs. Everyone is extremely nervous. The cannon is still rumbling in the distance.

And suddenly three nooses fall on three necks. These men have just enough time to shout with pride, with all their strength: "Goodbye comrades! Avenge us! Death to the executioners! Long live Stalin!"

## XVII. DIRECTED CACOPHONY

The tables are suddenly removed; the three inert bodies weigh on the stiffened ropes. The Germans break ranks, still at gunpoint. They are visibly relieved, seeing everyone disperse.

"And now play '*Deutsche Eichen*,'" shouts an SS man.

With the triumphant chords of this march, the meeting ends.

And it is still a day like so many others.

On a sunny summer afternoon, we play to entertain our guards, without even knowing if they can hear us because, at the same time, their radio is playing at its maximum volume. We play because we have to play. It is the overture to a German operetta.

Our flutist, the Doctor, is just playing a large-scale solo in which he puts all his energy, all his soul, perhaps to forget that he is there. He is so absorbed in his playing that he does not see the pattern of the trucks loaded with naked women passing on the road and heading towards the crematorium.

When the opening is over, the flutist puts his instrument down, happy with his performance.

The trucks have disappeared around a bend.

In one of them was the daughter of our flutist.

# XVIII. ROMANCES

After a period of indecision which was very beneficial to us, the Canada workforce was systematically managed and we found ourselves, to our great regret, assigned to a completely different kind of work.

The clothes that are too worn out, those of the dead or the sick, have to be disinfected so that they can be used again. From now on, we are responsible for collecting them from the barracks and transporting them to the huge red-brick building which serves as a sort of central lice stripping office. It is located so close to the crematorium and, moreover, it looks so much like them, that jokers advise us each time we go there not to make a mistake in our destination.

Since we are in constant contact with clothes and linens full of vermin, we have to subject our personal belongings and ourselves to a thorough disinfection on every trip. This is how we are mixed with groups of men and women who have escaped the screening of the arrival dock and who are simultaneously undergoing the hygiene protocol. As the days go by, these groups become more and more numerous, the services are overwhelmed and we are often turned away without disinfecting ourselves. Finally, one day we are told not to bring back our "merchandise" and are advised to go to the Gypsy Camp, where a similar office, of smaller dimensions, has recently been installed.

Established in March of 1943, the Gypsy Camp is strangely reminiscent of the old Czech camp. Children, women, old people and able-bodied men live in a community. But one essential difference offends the eyes of the layman.

The life of the gypsies, apparently a family life, is, in reality, an odious promiscuity. Dirt reigns supreme and contagious diseases spread to such an extent that half a dozen barracks are needed to set up a hospital ambulance for the sole use of the camp. The gypsies are

## XVIII. ROMANCES

systematically opposed to medical care and it is only when they can no longer stand that the sick consent to be hospitalized. Their hospital is nothing more than an antechamber to death.

The members of the same family live as parasites, one on top of the other. The fathers deprive the children and the women of their rations to exchange them for cigarettes or other fancies. The young, moreover, return the favor when the opportunity arises.

Gypsies are inveterate smokers. We frequently see boys and girls from eight to twelve years old smoking or begging for cigarette butts. The girls, in order to get cigarettes, prostitute themselves with the first bidder. There are some very pretty ones that cost up to ten cigarettes. There are also some that you can get for a more modest sum, one or two cigarettes, even for half a cigarette. Some have the reputation of being available for only one or two puffs.

This being known to all, many people want to take part in a chore in the gypsy camp. There was an official brothel in Auschwitz I for the use of prisoners, but not everyone was allowed to go there. Only those who were designated by the inspection service were allowed to go there periodically, taking turns. Therefore, the gypsy camp is overflowing with visitors of all kinds, and its appearance is singularly reminiscent of an oriental market.

By our frequent comings and goings, we soon become very popular with the gypsies. They know that we are the musicians who play in the morning and evening at the nearby camp, and they encourage us to get to know their musicians, who are quite numerous in the camp and who have their own instruments. Like ourselves, they often show off to their superiors, but they have only guitars and violins which cannot replace our saxes and brass instruments.

The chief of the disinfection barracks—with whom we constantly have to deal—is a German, an old convict, and a common law offender, who likes music a lot. He gave us the idea of bringing our own instruments on the day of his birthday, hiding them under the clothes we were carrying. In spite of the risk of such an enterprise, we decide to carry out this plan, even if it means disinfecting our instruments after the concert.

We manage to get our treasures out of our camp and into the gypsies' camp without a hitch. And here we are in the middle of a concert, in the midst of a large audience expressing its joy. All precautions have been taken, the SS on duty are in agreement, and it seems that we are in no danger.

Suddenly, in the middle of a jazz piece, we are terrified by the appearance of a man in a German uniform. This man is not unknown to us. During our participation in the work of Canada on the platforms of the station, we had many times had the opportunity to familiarize ourselves with the sinister silhouette of Mengele, the SS chief physician of the camp.

He is a handsome man of fairly high stature, with a hard, impenetrable gaze and the typical German officer's appearance. His aristocratic hands with elongated fingers would be the envy of many a high society woman. But the thumb of his right hand alone sums up an entire epic. The lives of millions of human beings have depended, for a split second, on a single movement of that graceful thumb. It is the *Lagerarzt* Mengele who supervises the human merchandise unloaded at Auschwitz.

A movement of the thumb to the right—and it is a life momentarily spared, in other words, destined for the camp. A movement to the left—and an immediate, irrevocable death sentence. But Dr. Mengele's thumb moves to the right only very rarely and reluctantly. The small gesture of this man condemns thousands of innocent people every day who only want to live like him.

When he appears, we stop playing and panic, wondering what he is doing there. The barracks leader, whose birthday we are celebrating,

## XVIII. ROMANCES

is the first to regain his composure and runs to Dr. Mengele to explain why we are here with the gypsies. Mengele listens to him with a distracted look on his face, his chin resting on the palm of his hand. He seems to be meditating on evil achievements. To our surprise, he beckons us to continue playing.

Since we have a singer in our midst, Bobby, who has some irresistibly funny numbers in his repertoire, we urge him to perform to cheer up our distinguished listener. And the miracle happens. Listening to our entertainer's boisterous fantasy, Mengele holds back with his hand the laughter that was about to burst forth and, as if constrained by his lack of willpower, he suddenly leaves without saying a word.

The day after the party, we learn the result of Mengele's visit to the gypsy camp. We will not go back there; we will never go again. The camp is confined. A quick census of the gypsies who have served in the German army is carried out and the able-bodied men are sent to an unknown destination. From our camp, we can see the heartbreaking scenes of farewell. Despite our familiarity with sudden and unusual events, we wonder why these men are being taken and where they are being taken.

Everything soon becomes clear. The gypsy mothers and wives will not have to suffer much longer from the abduction of their sons and husbands. Sequestered in our barracks, we can see, through a slit in the door, what is happening on the other side of the barbed wire.

Almost the entire SS force, reinforced by our Kapos with clubs, proceeded to load the gypsies onto trucks. The gypsies knew what awaited them, as opposed to those who went directly from freedom to the crematorium without suspecting where they were going. They offer fierce resistance. The Germans kept the able-bodied men away in order to reduce their resistance.

For two hours, shouts, screams, collective laments reach our ears. And then, calm returns. The trucks have left. The gypsy camp is deserted. All have been taken to the gas chambers.

As for the men who left during the day, we never heard of them again.

The gypsies had their own canteen. Now useless, it must be moved elsewhere. It is still the musicians who are in charge of the chore. We are happy to learn that the goods are to be taken to the women's camp.

We load our car with modest quantities of junk, arranging them in such a way as to make the load as voluminous as possible. This will allow us to save our strength and also to extend the duration of these trips, which we consider to be real fun.

The Germans have been showing some semblance of a desire to improve the condition of the female prisoners for some time. Water and electricity lines are installed in their homes, and various improvements are made that require constant visits by specialized workers, such as masons, cabinetmakers, locksmiths, glaziers and electricians. As was the case with the gypsies, there is no shortage of volunteers for this kind of expedition.

While most of the creatures in this camp bear little resemblance to what is generally understood by the word "woman," there are some attractive, pretty and even elegant ones. There is no lack of opportunities for men to approach them. Love affairs, more or less lasting, occur if you're one of the lucky ones. Letters and small parcels circulate daily in both directions, thanks to the complicity of those who are on duty. These connections extend on a vast scale, as if we had freedom. Sometimes it is an escapade without continuation, sometimes it is an adventure a little more prolonged, being favored by the sympathy of the "community" which does not ignore it. It is also, at times, a true passionate romance which, generated by a genuine love, is strengthened in a mutual spirit of revolt against the oppressor.

## XVIII. ROMANCES

We all know the story of the couple of prisoners who, after meeting each other, understanding and loving one another, decided to flee together. This was a heroic exploit, unprecedented in the annals of escapes. It took a long series of favorable circumstances, each of which, taken separately, was fraught with difficulties, to bring this challenge to the German organization to a successful conclusion.

To escape from the Auschwitz camp was simply an unfeasible undertaking and was doomed to failure. Even if you managed to break through the barbed wire fences or to escape from the outer camp, your absence was immediately reported and a real pack of SS men, inmates and trained dogs was sent after you. The ground was searched meter by meter, and sentries were alerted within a radius of forty kilometers. You could only try to escape at night, at the risk of being discovered by the watchtowers that were watching everywhere. During the day, you had to remain holed up in a more or less safe hiding place, and if you were not found the same day you escaped, the search was resumed on the following day until you were brought back, triumphantly, alive, riddled with bullets or dead. If you were still alive, you were hanged in public. If you were dead, you were put on a stool, with your back pressed against a shovel, to make you assume a sitting position, and a broomstick was slipped into your clenched hand, at the top of which was written, in fanciful characters, the cheerful inscription: "Hurrah! Here I am again!" And so you remained exposed for a day or two, in the most frequented place of the camp, to serve as a notice to your possible successors.

In spite of these manifestations of German humor, attempts to escape followed one after another. The successes were rare, and were always achieved with the help of an SS man who was bribed with money or jewelry.

This was the case with the couple in question.

On D-Day, the man entered the women's camp with an official task, but did not leave in the evening. Another man took his place, because at the checkpoint it was always the number that counted, not the individuals. A short time later, a military car entered the women's camp and took away the couple disguised as German officers. The car passed through the chain of sentries without a hitch and deposited them in a safe place. The two lovers were free and it was later known that the man had managed to take many secret documents with him.

The case was closed, the incident almost forgotten, when, after a few weeks, it bounced back. To our astonishment, the couple reappeared in Auschwitz, surrounded by guards, and we learned the tragic outcome of this novel.

They had lived in a Czech town in relative safety, never going out together, waiting for the opportunity to flee abroad, which would soon come. But one day, as they were walking on either side of the street, the Gestapo stopped the girl to ask for her papers. She had some prepared in advance, which seemed suspicious to the Germans, whom she had to follow to the chief's office. The man, believing his friend to be doomed, crossed the street without hesitation and presented himself before the Germans and asked to be arrested at the same time as her. It is only then that he learned that the suspicion of which his friend had been the object had nothing in common with their case and that, presumably, she would have been released after the interrogation.

The moving of the canteen, which could have been done in four days, has already been going on for three weeks. We are in no hurry to finish it. We go to the women's houses as many times a day as we want, often bringing back, in our car, objects that we have just transported there. The Germans seem to be less and less aware of the work that

## XVIII. ROMANCES

needs to be done, not only in our little improvised commando, but everywhere else.

Many of us now have our little flirtations at the nearby camp. If the poor doctor's daughter were alive, her father could see her every day and several times a day. Prostrate in his grief, he refuses, when he can, to participate in our excursions. On the other hand, his friend Michel never leaves us. His two sisters are always there and have recently become part of the women's orchestra, because, of course, there is an orchestra at the women's camp.

It was formed much later than ours, but it was created with the same purpose: to mark the entry and exit of the commandos. For a long time, the bass drum and cymbals alone formed the band, but little by little, with increased arrivals, a modest ensemble was formed, consisting of violins, mandolins, guitars and a cello. A few singers and even a grand piano, brought from who knows where, soon completed it. With time, it acquires a suitable repertoire composed, above all, of sweet music. This makes a happy contrast with the metallic sound of our trumpets, trombones and saxophones.

The two commanders of the respective camps even created a kind of rivalry between the two orchestras, each one praising the qualities of its "*Kapelle*." This led to some "cultural exchanges." One Sunday, our band gave a concert at the women's camp, the other Sunday, the women's ensemble came to be applauded at our camp.

This idyll was played out in peace, in parallel with the hangings and the constant arrival of new victims, two months after the Allied landings in Normandy and the front line being located only a hundred kilometers from us. At the same time as the first signs of the collapse of the Great German Reich reached us, the commandant of the women's camp intervened with our camp, requesting that one of our musicians come twice a week to give double bass lessons to a beginner, the instrument in question having just been "organized" by him. He is so firmly committed to enriching the sound of this delightful female ensemble! And, because of his tender solitude, the members of this orchestra lead a life absolutely different from ours.

The female musicians live in separate barracks, which is a rehearsal room with a small stage for individual performances. They are officially given extra food. Outside of the musical services, they do not work, they can devote themselves either to studies or to small personal works. The only thing they have in common with us is the obligation to take part in the selections, like all the other women.

The leader of this group, Alma Rosé,[9] a virtuoso violinist famous in Central Europe, is an excellent musician and an admirable companion.

Sensing that this might be a unique opportunity for her and her musicians to live decently, if not to survive, she spared no effort to get the German authorities to accept the need for her ensemble to exist. She knew how to stand up to the SS, defending her sick comrades threatened by the selections. After having saved more than one of them from the clutches of death, she herself had to be struck down by typhus.

Her baton, wrapped in crepe, is in the place of honor in the rehearsal hall.

---

9. Born November 8th, 1906 in Vienna. Deported to Auschwitz July 20th 1943 from the Drancy camp, number 50,381. Died in Birkenau in 1944, probably on June 4th. [Ed. note]

# XIX. SS AND SAINTE-CÉCILE

A foreigner passing through a small German town sees a brass band playing an aubade under the balcony of the town hall. To a passer-by, he asks: "Who is this concert for?"

"For our mayor, of course! It's his birthday."

"Why doesn't he show up on the balcony?"

"But because he is playing in the orchestra!"

This simplistic anecdote, which is widespread in Central Europe, innocently mocks the German's reckless love of music.

There is no doubt that every German is a born musician, and Auschwitz is still the most obvious proof of this.

Ever since we landed there, we have never stopped asking ourselves whether the German is a human being like all the others. Each time, the answer is categorical: "No, the German is not a man, the German is a *Kraut*, a monster, and what is more, a monster conscious of his monstrosity. He believes himself capable of doing what no one else will ever do. In the end, is he not right to proclaim his superiority over other races?"

When the German is under the influence of music, of "his" music, he begins to resemble any human being, as one usually imagines him. He does not shout, his voice is not guttural, his manner is gentle, he comes graciously to you with a friendly tap on the shoulder. Sometimes, when the air evokes in him a distant memory, he seems to think of his mother, his fiancée, and his eyes mist up with a moisture that looks strangely like human tears. It is at moments like these that we cannot help but hope that all is not lost for humanity, even if the Germans win the war. Are men who love music so much, men who cry while listening to it, capable of doing so much harm, of doing harm at all?

Alas! The charm dissipates as soon as the music stops. And the man reverts to what he really is: a *Kraut*, a monster.

For the duration of their performances, the musicians are virtually taboo. No performance can be interrupted while the SS is listening. Even the urgency of an order often proves to be ineffective. They would rather postpone the order rather than shorten their enjoyment. Their love of music is evident at every opportunity, and many of the SS men came to us in search of artistic recreation. But four of them especially honored us with their attention:

SS *Unterscharführer* Bishop[10] loves Jewish music. He is ashamed of his own perversity, but he can't help it, he is like a morphine addict who periodically demands his fix of the precious drug. We know his weakness, so we take all the necessary precautions when he visits. An available comrade is posted as a sentry at each door of the barracks to watch for and report an untimely arrival. It is then that the musicians play one after the other the favorite Jewish tunes of Bishop, and he is over the moon.

The session over, wanting to show his gratitude, he fumbles in his pockets, but most of the time he has forgotten his cigarettes. He borrows a pack from the clockmaker—without ever giving them back to him—and distributes them generously to the performers, while keeping the rest of the pack for himself.

After a long time of visiting us, SS *Unterscharführer* Bishop disappears one day. We learn that his fondness for Jewish music had been discovered and that he had been sent to the front.

SS *Sturmann* Baretzky[11] is also a music lover, but his repertoire is very limited. It merely consists in one march, "The German Oaks."

---

10. Born in 1904 in Essen, *Blockführer* in Birkenau (BIId). Not to be confused with Karl Bischoff, engineer, one of the builders of the crematoriums in Birkenau. [Ed. note]

11. Born in 1919 in Czernovitz, *Blockführer* in Auschwitz and Birkenau. He committed suicide in prison, where he was on remand, in 1988. [Ed. note]

## XIX. SS AND SAINTE-CÉCILE

So, once and for all, it is understood that the moment he appears at our sessions, outside or in the barracks, we must immediately attack the march in question, as the price of his great leniency towards us.

Baretzky is one of the greatest "terrors" of our camp. Eternally perched on his bicycle, he has no equal for bursting in wherever his presence is least needed.

His flair is unrivaled for "falling right on top" of the most delinquent cases and he is never short of refinements for an instantaneous sentence.

On Sunday we play our usual concert, not knowing that Baretzky is on duty. As we play a rather long overture, he bursts through the guardhouse window and stands motionless in the doorway. We continue our piece, believing that he is listening with pleasure.

Suddenly, just as we are about to begin the final allegro, Baretzky stops the music and quietly orders us to put on our work clothes and wait for him at the other end of the camp.

We do so, although we suspect that something bad is about to happen.

After a few minutes, he joins us on his bicycle. After leaning the machine against a tree, he orders us to line up in fives. Then he grabs a big stick, which he first swings gently for a few moments behind his back, and speaks to us, gradually increasing his voice, which becomes hoarse and bellowing:

"There is a lot of music in the world. For me, there is only one: my music. And my music is the march: 'The German Oaks!' You saw me earlier, at the window, and you didn't play it! You'll pay for that, my lads! Let's go! Let's go!"

And, brandishing his stick, he makes us carry out the most famous punishment in use in the German camps. While bearing a sympathetic and quite innocent name, it is the most terrible ordeal that a prisoner can undergo. It is called "playing sport."

In fact, it is a sport, but not a fun one at all. The strongest, most trained, most hardened athlete would hardly resist it for more than five minutes. Yet five minutes of "sport" is the minimum punishment in a camp. This is a benign and common punishment, although it is often the undernourished, defiant and even the "Muslims" who are subjected to it. The main movements are the following: running, bowing, standing up, jumping with bent knees, rolling on the ground, spinning around a pole with the head pressed against it, jumping into the water, climbing a steep hill, rolling down it, etc... All this alternated in a furious rhythm, without the slightest respite and under blows which occur at the smallest slackening or the slightest failure.

After a minute of this exercise, we sweat profusely, we pant like hunted beasts, our inhalation merges with exhalation, our ears ring, a sharp pain pierces our hearts, whose beats resemble rather the rolled tremolo of a drum. We anxiously ask ourselves how long Baretzky has set the "sport" to last. Five minutes? Ten minutes? We will never be able to keep up. Every second seems like an eternity.

Baretzky, unperturbed, his watch in hand, continues to rain down orders. The rhythm of the alternating exercises becomes ever faster. The movements follow one another and make the execution impossible. The blows fall harder. We jump like frogs, we crawl in the mud like reptiles, we cry with rage and impotence, we are mortified, degraded, humiliated, annihilated, reduced to the rank of abject vermin.

Baretzky consults his watch. Perhaps it is the end of our martyrdom? No, he goes on and on, watching especially those of us who, unable to move, try to cheat. Nothing escapes him, despite our numbers. It seems that it will never end.

Baretzky then makes a sign to stop the punishment and to announce that this time he wanted to show us his indulgence by inflicting us with only fifteen minutes of sport. Let's not forget it or it will be half an hour!

## XIX. SS AND SAINTE-CÉCILE

He then orders us to get back into our gala clothes and to continue the interrupted concert.

SS *Rottenführer* Broad is the best friend of our music. He is the head of the Political Bureau's annex, from which all decisions on individual or mass extermination of prisoners from all camps in Upper Silesia are made. Broad deals directly with the prisoners only when they are called to the Political Bureau for interrogation. Those who have been in front of him know that he has no equal in extracting from his interlocutor what he wants to know. But Broad's main function is to handle the files and cards containing all the relevant information on each detainee. When he pulls out a card and puts a special notation on it, it's an irrevocable death sentence.

This young man, no more than twenty-four years old, spends most of his leisure time in our musical sanctuary. He is highly educated and speaks several languages fluently. Nothing in his appearance betrays his macabre duties. It is with a cheerful air, as if detached from all earthly concerns, that he enters our home. It is like a visit to a university.

All SS men love music, but each one enjoys it in their own way. *Rottenführer* Broad could be classified as a professional virtuoso. His innate gifts as a musician and his extensive knowledge of music are evident in his every remark and every gesture. He is a first-rate performer, capable of taking his place in the best international ensembles.

His instrument is the accordion, the crude accordion. But it is under his fingers, fine and agile, artfully manipulating the keys and registers, that we understand all that this instrument is capable of rendering, when held by an accomplished performer. And it is thanks to him that we have been able to reconcile ourselves with this generally despised "orchestrion."

Broad is a lover of pure jazz. The entire repertoire, European and American, is familiar to him. And his choice of favorite pieces is proof of his refined taste. He enjoys playing with the best of our band and when he has the opportunity to innovate variations on the tune performed, it is a real treat for us. Sometimes he takes up the drums. Here again, his perilous rhythmic improvisations confirm the high opinion we have of his science and art.

Our accordions, samples of series, damaged by the bad weather, and not being able to satisfy Broad fully, cause him to bring his own one day. It is a magnificent new instrument, equipped with all the possible basses and with several registers. Its varnished wooden frame is strewn with small inlaid swastikas. Broad is an absolute master of his personal accordion and enjoys playing for us as a soloist, provoking our sincere admiration. But, as an ever-insatiable artist, he would like to add to his instrument an additional register that could imitate the sound of muted trumpets.

Our violin-clock-maker took on the task. For several weeks, he remained at work on Broad's accordion, hand-cutting all the parts needed to make the small levers and gears that operate this precision mechanism. When the work was finished, Broad, delighted, rewarded the craftsman with a generous gift: two hundred and fifty cigarettes.

Broad sometimes stays away several days without coming to see us. We know then that he is very busy. A few months ago, it was to select the women who were to form the staff of the brothel set up in Auschwitz I. Then it was to follow closely the development of the gypsy orchestra, of which he was the instigator.

Recently, his absence, which was more prolonged than the previous ones, was no small matter. It was a question of making ten thousand cards disappear, each one representing a gypsy, and of burning, the next day, the gypsies themselves, in identical number.

## XIX. SS AND SAINTE-CÉCILE

So when he told us about his overwork and fatigue, we understood perfectly the need for relaxation that SS *Rottenführer* Broad felt, as he sought to forget his daily worries in the chords of his instrument, enriched with an additional register.

SS *Unterscharführer* Wolff[12] belongs to the category of decent Germans. His manners are affable, he never gives us any official notice, and his frequent visits are those of a comrade who wants to amuse himself intellectually rather than those of a representative of authority.

Wolff has no preferences in his predilection for music. A popular polka moves him as much as a romance or a Christmas carol. So he spends long hours listening to what we play, without any special wishes as to the program, and chatting amiably with the clockmaker Heinz and André. The reason for these discussions is that SS and Heinz are both from the same town in Germany. This is a good pretext to evoke, on both sides, some memories. We witness the birth of a real camaraderie between SS *Unterscharführer* Wolff and the clockmaker Heinz Lewin, a Jewish detainee.

Every time Wolff returns from a few days' leave, Heinz asks him about his hometown. And, without seeming to notice that he is breaking the rule about fraternizing with prisoners, Wolff gives him a true account of his trip, as he would to a family member. He tells him that the city has suffered greatly from the Allied bombing, which continues unabated in all other German cities. He lists the streets, buildings and monuments that were particularly hard hit.

These talks often take place late at night and the outpourings

---

12. Born on July 23, 1910 in Lipsk. *Blockführer* and *Rapportführer* in the Birkenau camp in 1942/43. [Ed. note]

are encouraged. Little by little, the terrain of these conversations slips dangerously towards the problems that have never ceased to torment us.

Wolff is certainly not a Nazi like many others. If he is a servant of Hitler, if he adores him, if he obeys him, he does not make him his god, nor his religion. He obviously considers him a man of genius, but not without failures, who is undoubtedly destined to play a decisive role in the history of humanity.

One evening, Heinz risks a question that we all have permanently on our lips. It is at a time when a state of alert has been declared in Germany. The *Volkssturm* has just been promulgated, "the fatherland is in danger." One would think that Wolff would consider the subject matter to be beyond the bounds of propriety, and that he would, as all Nazis do, hide behind the wall of National Socialist faith that does not admit of any argument. Yet, no, the SS Wolff does not dodge the question. On the contrary, he allows himself to be drawn into a real "interview," guessing the hidden meaning of the words and getting to the bottom of the problem, as usual.

"Do you think," Heinz asks, "that Germany will win the war?"

"Not precisely," Wolff replies, after a moment's reflection.

"And if the war is lost... what has happened, what is happening here, in our camp, will one day be known to the whole world... then perhaps you will be called to account?"

"No one will ever know anything," Wolff says with a smile. "We will not be called to account."

"Yes, I understand, you mean that there will be no witnesses..."

"Oh, no, that's not what I mean."

A silence follows. Wolff seems to be gathering his thoughts, weighing the words he must say. And he continues, as if with regret:

"After all, perhaps it is better that you know the truth. You see, in principle, you are not mistaken: theoretically speaking, there should be no witnesses capable of telling the world about the things that have taken place in Auschwitz."

"But what is essential is that, even if there are witnesses and they speak, *they will not be believed by anyone.* This is the genius of our Führer. He has done something very simple, but which is precisely super-genius in its simplicity. He has conceived and realized that which seems unattainable to the mere mortal. What is the use of wasting precious time in assimilating the rest of mankind to the National Socialist faith? Wouldn't it be simpler to eliminate these backward minds, starting with the weakest and ending with the strongest? I realize that this sounds 'monstrous' to you. But that is because you are not of our race. You call the acts we commit here 'crimes.' But don't forget that these acts are done in a time of war, in an isolated corner specially chosen for this purpose, separated from the rest of the world by a solid cordon of barbed wire and sentries. Everything that happens here will always remain hidden from the eyes of the curious and, therefore, forever ignored by the public consciousness. Even if we lose the war, we will not be presented with a 'bill.' Your judgment, if there is one, will be made in a public tribunal, in broad daylight, on the basis of a penal code that will no longer be equal to the 'offenses' committed. Your judges will therefore be led to declare themselves incompetent. No 'human' justice can punish arbitrariness with arbitrariness. At most, the great leaders will have to justify themselves. But Germany will always live..."

# XX. DECRESCENDO

The war, which until now was only an abstract thing for us, is getting closer and closer. All around, everything seems to announce it and the signs are more and more favorable every day.

The German army needs reinforcements and the SS personnel is gradually being reduced. When we arrived, there were more than two thousand of them. At the moment, there are less than two hundred. The authorities have tried to compensate for this shortage by recruiting SS men of Ukrainian origin. But as a result of the massive number of escapes, the recruitment of non-German elements had to be abandoned. The gaps have been eventually filled by older men from the *Volkssturm* and retired police officers. Naturally, these men, having undergone neither the training nor the compulsory tests of SS officers, don't have either their mentality nor their moral standards. When they can, they proclaim, with ostentation, that they are SS only by their uniform.

Anti-aircraft artillery has recently taken up position in the immediate vicinity of the camp. It is engaged in intensive training. Live-fire exercises are conducted day and night, and we often wonder whether these maneuvers are intended to cover the distant but audible sounds of Soviet guns.

And then, suddenly, we come into direct contact with the war—such exaltation!

American and Russian planes burst into the sky over Auschwitz. The same sirens that signaled the escape of a prisoner with a unified roar, with a repeated mournful crescendo and decrescendo, now announce to us that the alert has been given. We are then prescribed a severe instruction. All the commandos must, at the sound of the alarm, return immediately to the camp. This, of course, is to prevent escaping in case of panic or bombing. We are ordered to stay in the barracks for the duration of the alert. However, overflowing with joy, we prefer to

## XX. DECRESCENDO

expose ourselves to punishment rather than deprive ourselves of the pleasure of contemplating the flight of these silver machines which, for us, are the long-awaited messengers of our deliverance.

We almost openly disregard the order, standing outside to follow with attention the movements of the airplanes to which we wave our welcome. We hear the detonation of the bombs dropped on the Auschwitz train station and the SS barracks. And when we later learn that there were several dozen victims among the prisoners, we are sure that they died with joy for a good cause.

Apparently, the general mobilization of the *Volkssturm* is insufficient to stop the flow of the Allied armies. The quasi-voluntary recruitment of non-political German prisoners, i.e. holders of green triangles, is now being carried out. About sixty of them present themselves at the urgent call of the routed army. Their departure is a great event in the camp. We play as they gather, we precede them with music to the disinfection area, we play the songs they ask for while they are washing in the shower room, and finally we accompany them to the train that is to take them away.

We were to learn later that their enrollment has not changed the course of events. Intoxicated by freedom, which they no longer knew how to use, they killed each other to settle old scores, even before reaching the front line.

The conditions of life in the camp change from minute to minute. The official instructions undergo significant about-faces.

It is now forbidden to beat the prisoners. All corporal punishment must be preceded by a detailed report with the approval of the authorities.

As the construction of a military hospital to receive the wounded from the front is started, the hygiene of the prisoners is improved by the installation of water pipes and toilets in each of the barracks.

The SS are visibly panicked. In an attempt to gain sympathy among the Jewish internees, they try to absolve themselves of responsibility for their past actions and blame their superiors and even the Berlin office. Many of them, having once provided German uniforms to the escapees, now try to "organize" civilian clothes and stripes in secret, with the obvious purpose of mingling with their victims if the need arises.

Escapes are becoming more and more numerous, especially among Russian prisoners. Most of them succeed. The Beskid mountain range, which we can see to the south, is full of partisans who, with the help of reliable accomplices, are able to build up an underground network that the escapees can follow in complete safety. The avalanche of escapes does not diminish despite the hangings and collective punishments. The acts of resistance multiply inside the camp and the SS seem to be completely powerless.

After slipping away, the commandant reappears among us, bearing a strange message.

One afternoon, we are suddenly ordered off a wood chore and told to return to the camp to play for the commandos who have returned much earlier than usual. This influx of orders and counterorders has become commonplace.

Everything goes on as usual. The commandos march impeccably to the rhythm of our music. Since the recent orders came into effect, there are hardly any dead bodies or even cripples among the inmates returning from work.

After our last march, we are about to leave our podium, when we are told to stay put by the SS pavilion. At the same time, Schwarzhuber appears.

The person who is walking towards us is no longer the impeccable military-looking figure. Schwarzhuber is metamorphosed. He walks with difficulty, staggers in wide curves and stumbles against imaginary

## XX. DECRESCENDO

obstacles with every step. In fact, he is completely drunk. A few SS non-commissioned officers and soldiers follow him a few steps away, respectfully. With the impatience of a spoiled child, he tells them to go away and take roll call.

Taking the conductor's baton, he then commands us, with a mocking sneer, to play his beloved tune, "*Heimat, deine Sterne*" and directs us as well as a drunken SS can. From afar, the internees and the Germans alike observe this scene with half-amused, half-shocked curiosity. We play with our usual conscientiousness and make it to the end of the piece without incident. We are amazed when Schwarzhuber asks us point-blank: "Can you play me 'The Internationale?'"

Stunned, none of us know how to react. Should we laugh and thus imply that we have understood the joke? Should we be offended? Should we remain silent? Lucien is the first to come to his senses. He stands at attention and says:

"We don't have the music, *Herr Lagerführer*."

"And why don't you have it yet?" Schwarzhuber says, with the obstinacy of a drunkard. Then he adds, suddenly calmed down: "It doesn't matter, you'll have it soon." Then, handing back his baton, he walks away, still wobbling on his legs, towards the interior of the camp.

The roll call takes place in deadly silence. Not the slightest change in the usual protocol. The SS check the number of prisoners and report to the *Rapportführer*. At his command, we all stand still as one man, taking off our headgear with the traditional clap. We wait, motionless, for the *Rapportführer* to greet the commandant, raise his right hand, and utter the sacramental "*Heil Hiltler*," which is still in force, before respectfully announcing that the number of people present is strictly in accordance with the number in the file office.

Contrary to our expectation, we don't break ranks once the ceremony is over, because, we are told, the commander has an important message to deliver.

Indeed, we soon see him stop in front of the first barracks where he begins to make a speech. When he is finished, cheers burst from the ranks of the prisoners. The same operation is repeated at each of the barracks. Finally, here he is in front of us.

Two interpreters accompany him and translate his sentences as they are spoken. The words of our commandant seem to intoxicate him further. He staggers more and more, his elocution is laborious, although he repeats the same sentences as those pronounced in front of the others. He is always trying to figure out what he is going to say, makes mistakes, clumsily repeats himself several times. It is as if he wanted to convince us of something he does not believe himself.

"Detainees!"—he begins solemnly—"Detainees, don't let yourselves be defeated! Do not believe the so-called alarming news that is reported to you by thoughtless elements! Do not let yourselves be demoralized by the alerts, nor by the bombardments, nor by the noise of the cannons! You are obviously too far from the theater of operations to form a correct opinion of the situation. The ingenious strategy of our Führer has led him to let the enemy penetrate our territories in order to provoke in him a false joy that will contribute to his final loss! We will let him come to the Bug[13] and there we will stop him! If he tries to get past us, well, we'll use asphyxiating gas. Prisoners! Do not lose courage! Observe discipline more than ever, do not try to escape, because sooner or later you will be caught and punished! Here you are perfectly safe. Those of you who will conduct yourselves in an exemplary manner will soon be released. Long live Germany! Long live our Führer!"

And, under the acclamations and "hurrahs!," Schwarzhuber leaves us to continue his round and thus complete the order that he has, no doubt, received directly from Berlin.

---

13. A major river in Central Europe that flows through Belarus, Poland, and Ukraine.

## XX. DECRESCENDO

The purpose of this harangue is achieved. Our morale is raised. We are comforted. In truth, we are exultant. The dawn of revenge is rising.

# XXI. SEVENTH OF THE DOMINANT

The Germans are definitely not sparing any means to save the compromised situation. A significant change in our lives has taken place unexpectedly. Could this be a new proof of that sublime strategy of the Führer of which Schwarzhuber spoke of in his speech? In any case, the fact is there: André has been removed from his position as conductor and Franz Danisch is responsible for this. Having caught wind about a music session that André had organized secretly for some Russians and Poles, he denounced him to the authorities and then, using the pretext of the disastrous influence of his music on the morale of the prisoners, obtained that Lucien replace him.

We undergo the ensuing reforms with an amused stupor.

A convinced pessimist and having come to terms, like all of us, with the idea of ending his days in the camp, Lucien considers his appointment as a just outcome of his career. His first concern is to provide us with superb white suits with wide red stripes down the middle of the back and on the sides of the pants. He also replaces André's thin rod with an imposing black baton. We don't always understand the pompous, curving movements that the latter outlines in Lucien's hand, but they provoke openly expressed joy in the Germans. Our repertoire also undergoes variations. Lucien acquires a collection of songs for the German troops, as well as several popular hits. So we play only polka marches, foxtrot marches, tango marches and, to crown the series, we end with "On a Persian Market," thus showing the path to follow for the glorious army of the Great Reich.

While our traveling circus parades are going on, the most unbelievable rumors are circulating. The more unbelievable they are, the more trustworthy they seem to us.

## XXI. SEVENTH OF THE DOMINANT

The latest rumor is that the partisan army is ready to come down from the mountains to deliver us, in conjunction with a parachuted Soviet corps.

Moreover, two wagons full of handcuffs have just arrived at the Auschwitz station. They are intended for us. Since the camp has to be evacuated by our own means, it would not be possible for us to escape with our hands chained along the way.

At the same time, from a so-called "reliable" source, we learn that the radio has issued a statement that we will be exchanged for German prisoners of war at the rate of two prisoners for one German.

According to the latest news, the SS should be leaving our camp for good, to be replaced by the *Wehrmacht* representatives in charge of repatriating us.

All this because the transports stopped arriving a few days ago. Because, to our astonishment, the chimneys of the crematorium are now idle and look like dimmed lamps. We build up all kinds of hopes: the Germans have lost, the military situation is catastrophic, there will never be another supply of human flesh brought to the sleeping furnaces.

And once again, as if to crush our faith, an avalanche of victims is poured onto the docks. The sky is once again covered with black smoke.

Where can these unfortunates still come from? We learn, with what anguish, that they come from camps closer to the front line than ours.

Our only consolation is the fact that the convoys now consist only of open wagons, betraying the haste with which the Germans are evacuating the area.

However, this time, these are the last transports. The musicians are the first to realize this.

The people of the Special Commando have done a good job and deserve a reward. We receive the order to dress up: we have to give a big concert. Contrary to usual routine, we are not told where we have to go and play. All we know is that our concert will take place outside the camp.

We line up and head for the exit. There, a disturbing surprise awaits us. We are surrounded by half a dozen SS men and led, to the sound of our own music, towards the crematorium! Full of horror and deathly pale, we ask ourselves the same question: we are going in, but will we get out alive?

In the courtyard, benches are already arranged, around which stand small groups of prisoners. At the sign of the SS, we sit on the benches and play among our comrades whom the Germans have forced for years to gas and burn their brothers. We play, knowing that this music will be their last pleasure on earth. They know it too. This favor of an hour's entertainment, generously granted by the Germans, has a price. This is their usual procedure. It is not the first time that they have resorted to this kind of charity prior to assassination.

When the concert is over, the miserable wretches shower us with gifts. We refuse them, but they urge us to take them, saying with sadness: "Take it, it can still be useful, we won't need it anymore."

A few days later, we are told that the men in the crematorium did not want to wait for their death. An uprising broke out in their enclosure, the guards were killed, the sinister building was set on fire by its occupants who fled in all directions. The SS, enraged by this unprecedented insolence, intervened savagely, mobilizing all the means at their disposal, caught up with almost all the fugitives and shot them on the spot.

The moment so hoped for, so feared too, has finally arrived. The evacuation of the camp begins. The prisoners are gathered in the square for a first sorting.

## XXI. SEVENTH OF THE DOMINANT

We would like to know what was behind the first choices made, and how they were made. Is it by nationality, by profession, by age, or even by seniority of the prisoners that one proceeds? But clues are unavailable. It is always the same German method, cleverly disorganized and trying to leave us unaware of our fate until the end.

The barracks are gradually emptying. Our orchestra is still intact and everything leads us to believe that we will be the last ones the Germans will want to part with. What we fear above all is the dispersion of our fellow musicians. We would like to stay together until the end of our odyssey. Having shared our miseries and joys for so long, we have come to form a kind of close-knit community, and we think that by staying close together we will have more courage to face the final hardships that await us.

Will we leave? Will we not leave? Perhaps the Germans will abandon us at the last moment? While waiting for events to answer our questions, we are undergoing a real war of nerves. We pack and unpack several times a day. Each of us has small personal possessions, "organized" with great difficulty and which we want to take with us. We were all able to pick up a few provisions. I myself was able to put together a sewing kit, scissors, needles, thread, which has served me well and which I don't want to part with at any price. Lucien's box contains paper and colored pencils: he hopes that his drawings will help him get by everywhere. André contemplates with melancholy the piles of scores written in his hand and which must be abandoned. But the most annoyed of all is, without doubt, the clockmaker. He is constantly sorting and rearranging his tools according to their usefulness and size, even if it means taking only the bare necessities with him at the last moment.

The camp is more and more depopulated and our barracks is almost empty. The carpenters are gone, the firemen are gone, the electricians are gone, only the orchestra is still there, as well as our barracks leader, Joseph Hoffmann. This good and brave German, a former police employee from a district of Breslau, arrested for being involved in a black market, is a fervent patriot. He has never stopped proclaiming the infallibility of the German army and still cries out to us, despite his fifty-six years, his regret at not being able to join the ranks of this army where a hundred men like him would "whip the red hordes."

Not a day goes by without his announcing a new and ever more formidable German secret weapon, without his telling us that the days of the Allies are numbered. His triumphant air never leaves him, especially when he is the bearer of a pernicious piece of information, no matter whether it applies to him or us.

Hoffmann is now the only point of contact with the outside world and we are entirely dependent on this one source of information.

We have no chores to do and everyone is busy in his own way. Some of us try to "organize" a little more food, others make backpacks, and finally, a few devotees stay at home to play some music and thus forget the turmoil.

Hoffmann multiplies his false news. Sometimes we have to leave all together, the same day, sometimes we all have to stay, the SS will abandon us, the Russians are in sight. An hour later, he tells us that we must take our instruments with us and recommends that we clean them well.

We are weary and we end up not paying any more attention to his announcements and wait for events to happen, with total resignation.

# XXII. FINAL CHORD

The *Musikstube* is today the center of an intimate and strange activity. Most of the musicians have gathered there to listen to the performance of a string quartet. We have forgotten the barbed wire, the Germans, the war. We no longer think about the fate that awaits us, nor about our misery. We have become normal people again for the short time that the music lasts, and we listen to it in religious contemplation. We can see, through the windows, Hoffmann running around, but we only think of enjoying the celestial harmonies of the quartet. While the notes of the fourth part are being played, we think that these may be the last measures we will hear on earth.

The enchantment is over. We are still under the effect of the last chords when Hoffmann enters and shouts triumphantly:

"Didn't I tell you? Everyone is leaving, today!"

We are still in doubt. But this time Hoffmann is telling the truth. An SS man comes along and confirms it.

Relief follows the confusion. At last, we know for sure. We leave.

I take one last look at our beautiful music room where our instruments are impeccably arranged and, grabbing my pack, I join my comrades who are gathering in the courtyard. Even during the liquidation of the camp, the hygiene protocol is still in effect. We are instructed to go to the disinfection room, to get rid of our linens and clothes and to get "clean" ones. Only our shoes are returned to us.

We are disinfected and dressed again. Dressed in awful clothes taken at random from the pile, we are transformed into a herd of rags, after having been for so long a model of cleanliness and elegance. We look at each other and can hardly recognize each other. If some take it with good humor, others suffer terribly from this sudden decline. For Lucien, it is a real fall from grace. Just two hours ago, he was a leading figure of the camp, a lord, tall, handsome, imposing in stature and full of confidence. I have before me now a little old man, cowering, without courage, without morale, and who, as the events unfold, sees only a tragic end to his career. As for André, he is still the same, calm and level-headed, but a thin smile hangs on the corner of his lips, a smile whose meaning I think I can guess. The turning point of our destiny is at the same time the turning point of History. It doesn't matter what our fate is, as long as humanity is victorious.

Before leaving the camp, we look at the long row of barracks, the central alley that we walked along with our instruments, or followed with our car, the extinguished chimneys of the crematoriums, and we see the ghosts of millions of engulfed human beings standing before us, invoking their martyrdom and begging for a merciless vengeance.

On our way to the train station, where we are to be taken to an unknown destination, we pass a small group of SS officers. Our commander is among them. He does not recognize us until we take off our caps to greet him one last time. His face becomes more serious. He turns to his colleagues and exclaims with a mixture of pride and melancholy, *"Meine schöne Kapelle!" (My beautiful band!)*

At the last moment, André has managed to "organize" two loaves of bread and two sausages. He takes a bite and says to me, "Oh well, we'll have to start again."

Piled on top of each other in a sealed wagon car, we are driving towards our new destiny, towards a new unknown. Next to us, Dimitri struggles in the bumpy train to sort out a collection of cigarette butts, the last ones he was able to pick up. Bronek has settled in a corner and is trying to protect his sick leg from being jostled. Lucien tries in vain to exercise his extinguished authority over his musicians who are no longer his. The Doctor and Michel are also there, inseparable as

## XXII. FINAL CHORD

always. The two sisters of the latter were evacuated a few days before, no one knows where.

We drive towards the West…

"Oh well, we'll have to start again." Indeed, it was to be a new beginning.

Dispersed along the way, we are to be assigned, in small groups, to various transit camps and to flee, with the Germans and in spite of ourselves, before the "enemy" at our heels. Many months will pass before the most miraculous of miracles will take place and before we are able to see our torturers be made prisoners by their former prisoners.

When I evoke Auschwitz and the monstrous extermination of peoples which fate made me witness, I can only note the little importance of my own peregrinations. I am a castaway in an immense catastrophe, and my life is of no importance except to those closest to me and to myself. But, however little it may represent, I cannot help thinking that I owe it to one factor only: the German's reckless love for music.

And I will always remember the words of farewell, full of pain and regret, which the *Lagerführer* of Auschwitz-Birkenau gave us when we left:

"*Meine schöne Kapelle!*"

# André Laks
# ABOUT MY FATHER

*In memory of Antoni Buchner (1944-2014)*
*and Amaury du Closel (1956-2024)*


My father Simon Laks was a composer. As a member of the *Association des Jeunes Musiciens Polonais* (Association of Young Polish Musicians) founded in Paris in 1926, he was close to the so-called *École de Paris* (Paris School)[1] which before the war brought together young composers from the East, such as Bohuslav Martinu, Marcel Mihalovici, and Alexander Tansman, of whom he became a friend. He left behind a work of quality, clearly marked by the French school, with its meticulous concern for formal construction and tonal refinement, but he was also strongly rooted in the traditions of Poland and influenced by contemporaries like Szymanowski, to whom he dedicated his *Suite Polonaise* (Polish Suite). In 1964, in an interview with musicologist Tadeusz Kaczyński, he said that he was not sure that his work would survive, except for his songs.[2] The recent rediscovery of his instrumental work, in circumstances I will mention later, suggests that he was mistaken. Born in Warsaw on November 1, 1901, he moved to Paris in 1926 to complete his musical studies and began his career there. He was interned in the Beaune-la-Rolande camp from May 14,

---

1. For the label "École de Paris" and the position of Simon Laks in Parisian musical life during the interwar period, see the essay by Frank Harders-Wuthenow *Écoles de Paris - Paris pour École* in the booklet of the recording of Laks' *Concerto da camera* which can be downloaded from the EDA records website.

2. The interview, originally published in the Polish magazine *Ruch Muzyczny* ("The Musical Movement"), September 1964, number 21, is available in a French translation in *Mélodies d'Auschwitz et autres écrits sur les camps* (Cerf, 2028), pp. 364-72. This is one of the few texts where my father, who did not like to talk about himself, talks a little about his music.

1941 to July 16, 1942 as a foreign Jew, then deported on July 17, 1942 by convoy 6 to Auschwitz II-Birkenau, where he received the number 49,543. His two brothers Henry (1897-1989) and Léo (1906-1966), who came to France at about the same time, escaped deportation by taking refuge in the southern zone near Nice. The third brother, David, also a musician, died in the Warsaw ghetto (1906-1942).[3] His parents, as well as a sister, Hannah, and her son Edzio, who had remained in Poland, perished in the Nazi camps (most probably in Treblinka).[4]

It was his musical skills that saved my father from the death to which he was destined. He was first a member (violinist), then conductor of the Auschwitz-Birkenau orchestra. The role of music for my father in Auschwitz is the object of the two books I will talk about in a moment.

After the liberation of the camp, he returned to Paris. He became a French citizen in 1948 and in 1949 he married my mother, whom he had met in 1947. She had survived the war by hiding in Warsaw under the name of Paulina Rudowska (Finkielkraut was her real name) and had chosen to settle in France, while her sister Maria, who had spent the war in France, returned to build socialism.

My father died in Paris on December 11, 1983, in the apartment on Rue de Chazelles where I was born in 1950. My mother, born in 1910 (she made herself younger on her false papers, declaring May 1$^{st}$ 1912), died there on September 23$^{rd}$ 2001.

*Musiques d'un autre monde* is the title of the book that was published in 1948 under the two names of René Coudy and Simon

---

[3]. I was unaware of his existence until the exhibition "Musik in okkupierten Polen (Music in occupied Poland) 1939-1945", which was curated by Katarzyna Naliwajek-Mazurek and opened on July 13, 2010 in Kiel as part of the Schleswig-Holstein Music Festival "Polen im Puls." A document from the Warsaw Conservatory of Music dated 1929 gives his date of birth as 1906. It seems that he was Leo's twin.

[4]. See my father's Polish book « *Szargam świętości* » (*Profanation of the Holy)*, London 1980, p. 67.

Laks by Mercure de France, and which tells the story of their survival in the camp. It was prefaced by Georges Duhamel, a renowned voice at that time.[5] In the 1970s, my father wrote a revised version in Polish. After an unsuccessful attempt to publish it in Poland, the book finally came out in 1979 by a small Polish publisher in London—the *Oficyna Poetów i Malarzy* (*Poets' and Painters' Press*)—which played a prominent role in the dissemination of Polish emigrant literature under the Communist regime.[6] The Polish text was republished in 1998 by the Auschwitz-Brzezinka Museum Publishing House (*Panstwowe Museum Oświęcim-Brzezinka*).

After my father's death, I made sure that the Polish version was translated. An English version existed, by Chester K. Kisiel, a bilingual Polish speaker from Warsaw, who had spontaneously undertaken it. Jonathan Brent, who edited a history series at Northwestern University Press, and to whom I presented the project at an academic event in Washington in early 1988, expressed interest and published the book in 1989, which was unfortunately given the title of the first 1948 book.[7] It was also quickly translated into Dutch by Jos den Bekker and published by Kritak in Leuven under the title *Kapelmeester van Auschwitz*. I owe the first publication in French (1991) by the Éditions du Cerf, in a translation by Laurence Dyèvre, to Heinz Wismann. The most difficult case was Germany. The market, several potential publishers told me, was saturated with memoirs about the Holocaust. The publication by Droste Verlag (*Musik in Auschwitz*, 1997, translated by Mirka and Karlheinz Machel) is the result of the energy and commitment of Teda Wellmer. I am indebted to her and to the Fritz Bauer Institute

---

5. See Annette Becker's contribution in this volume, p. 172-175.
6. The house was run by Krystyna and Czesław Bednarczyk, with whom my father maintained a long friendship and correspondence, now edited by Jadwiga Malik (*Szymon Laks Krystyna i Czesław Bednarczykowie. Korespondencja*, Cracovia, Avalon 2018). The work results form a master thesis written under the direction of Prof. Janusz Gruchała in 2017.
7. See above the Editorial Note.

in Frankfurt, which supported her efforts and the publication. There is also a Spanish version of the book, in a translation by Xavier Farré, available from Herder (Mexico City, 2018).[8]

Explaining why he wanted to rewrite the 1948 book, my father notes in the Preface ("Overture") of the 1979 version: "Fate decreed that I has to take up this work alone and decide for myself what to leave in, what to take out, and what to change from the perspective of the past decades."[9] I think he had lost contact with René Coudy very early on after the book was published; I know that at the time my father was thinking of rewriting the book in Polish, he searched for him, in vain.[10] I hope not to offend René Coudy's memory by reporting here what my father once told me, namely that Coudy had been more of a second-in-command than a literary collaborator. This probably explains why my father felt authorized to sign with his name alone a book whose material remains basically the same. But there are cuts, additions, changes in the approach and in the form: In the 1948 version, each chapter bears a musical title–Alla tedesca, Invitation to the Muse, First Sounds, Fragile Consonances, Decrescendo, etc.—like the chapters of Primo Levi's *Periodic System* (*Il Sistema periodico*, 1975), which are each named after an element.[11] Moreover, while in *Mélodies d'Auschwitz* my father speaks of himself in the first person, the "I" in *Musiques d'un autre*

---

8. The version published in Madrid by Arena Libros in 2008 is definitively replaced by this publication, which also contains the translation of *Musiques d'un autre monde* (1948) as well as a previous version of the three essays by Annette Becker, Frank-Harders Wuthenow and myself published in the present volume.

9. *MA,* p. 6 (see above the Editorial Note).

10. Two letters that he sent to him in January 1973 and February 1974 returned with the mention "does not live at the address indicated". René Coudy was still alive at the time, contrary to what I have assumed in the past (see my postface to *Mélodies d'Auschwitz et autres écrits sur les camps*, Éditions du Cerf 2018, p. 326, n.2 and Annette Becker in the present volume, p. 189, n. 83).

11. The comparison had been initiated by Pierre Vidal-Naquet in the preface he wrote for the French edition of *Mélodies d'Auschwitz* (Cerf, 2004), cf. Editorial Note, above p. 8, Footnote 2.

*monde* is René Coudy, whereas my father is André (the name he was to give me two years later): "André is the real complete musician, and the entirety of his competence is revealed at each opportunity. Without a piano—in fact, we don't have one—he is able to harmonize and orchestrate any piece of music, often making do with a vocal line that is provided to him. Or, if a vocal line is not available, reconstructing the music from memory. He is in charge of writing all the orchestrations for our music, directing the rehearsals, and working out all the details of the performance." René Coudy played the saxophone.

As I mentioned above, the Polish authorities, whom my father had contacted for a possible publication in Poland, rejected the project. The reason given was that the book gave a "too idyllic" representation of the executioners. The reproach is absurd, of course. It is probably based on the fact that the text, written in a rather cold style, like the 1948 version, deliberately avoids, as far as possible, the description of the horrors of the camp, which are explicitly presupposed.[12] The books explore the privileged link between Germans and music, and more specifically the relationship between Nazi barbarism and German culture. This relationship is symbolized, in the 1979 version, by the stop of the convoy 6 at the station of Eisenach, which is the birthplace of Johann Sebastian Bach: "Such was my first encounter with music during my deportation."[13]

Michael Pollak, in his book *L'Expérience concentrationnaire: essai sur le maintien de l'identité sociale* (Paris, 1990), described the extreme difficulty, among the survivors, of speaking out, to say the unspeakable, and to accept oneself.[14] For survival in the extermination camps was

---

12. See also the letter to Krystyna Żywulska translated in *Mélodies d'Auschwitz* (Cerf, 2018), p. 339-41.
13. Cf. *AM*, p. 20.
14. The first part of Pollack's book, which reports and comments on the narratives from three survivors of the Auschwitz-Birkenau women's camp, is titled " La gestion de l'indicible" ("Managing the Unspeakable.") As Annette Becker points out, historians now take into account not only what could not be said, but also what could not be heard.

often linked to the occupation of privileged positions, and thus to one form or another of collaboration with the executioners. The desire to testify is thus inextricably mixed with the impossibility of doing so, or of doing it all the way through, out of simple self-respect.[15] One can see in the reserve, and even the irony, that characterizes both of my father's books on Auschwitz as a manifestation of the necessary distance that some witnesses had to take in order to testify.

After describing Auschwitz as a kind of "'negative' of the world which we had left" where "white became black and black white, values were turned around 180 degrees," so that the choice was "either to beat and torture" one's neighbors, or "to be beaten and tortured by him," my father says in 1979 that he "did not have to get rid of a single ordinary human virtue" in order to survive."[16] One can ask, however, whether occupying a 'prominent' position in the camp is it not by itself a compromise. What is certain is that a musician was in a better position than a doctor or a nurse in the *Revier*, whose ethics were challenged every minute, not to speak a Kapo or a member of the *Sonderkommando*.

Written almost 30 years after the French *Musiques d'un autre monde* (1948), the Polish *Mélodies d'Auschwitz* (1979) aims to not only be more objective (in fact, a few hints that were still felt to be unnecessarily pathetic or too "subjective" have been removed); the book also takes a stand in relation to other survivors' accounts that have appeared in the meantime, and to the opinions expressed in the specialized literature on the function of music in the camp.

Music in Nazi concentration and extermination camps is not a homogeneous phenomenon. It was sometimes used as a cultural

---

15. Pollak, *op. cit.,* p.179f., and above all 183f.
16. Cf. *AM,* p. 17f. In the deposition collected by the Commission on the History of World War II stored at the Institute for the History of the Present Time as DII—376, my father says: "It was impossible to practice in the concentration camp a moral of sacrifice." (The sentence is quoted by Pollak, *op. cit.*, pp. 193f.)

"showcase", like in Terezin. It could serve sadistic purposes.[17] In Auschwitz, music was partly a cog in the organization of camp life (the function of the orchestra was essentially to accompany the exits and returns from work), and partly served to entertain the executioners. Could it constitute, in certain circumstances, an act of resistance? Aleksander Kulisiewicz, who, as my father relates at the beginning of his 1979 book, was working to "collect songs, poetry, and music from the camps in general, in all its forms," thought so, and visited my father in 1974, looking for material. My father must have disappointed him. In Auschwitz at any rate, music was an instrument in the hands of the oppressor, not the victims. In an article entitled, "Camp Music and Camp Songs: Szymon Laks and Aleksander Kulisiewicz,"[18] David H. Hirsch suggests that the reason why Kulisiewicz and my father had different perceptions and interests on the question of music in the camps may have had something to do with the fact that one was a Jew, and therefore virtually condemned to death, while the other, a political prisoner, was not, which may have been a factor of hope. It seems rather that it could have been so here and so differently elsewhere.[19]

My father was a composer by profession. Auschwitz was an episode that has little to do with music, the real thing. My friend Karl Grob, in an unfortunately unpublished text, has emphasized this point by drawing a clear distinction between "living for music" and "living by means of music" a distinction inspired by my father's

---

17. See Paul Celan 's "Fugue of Death."
18. In *Confronting the Holocaust: A Mandate for the 21st Century*, edited by G. Jan Colijn et Marcia Sachs Littell, Lanham, MD : University Press of America, 1997, p. 157-168. There is a correspondence between my father and A. Kulisiewicz in the archives of the Memorial Holocaust Museum in Washington. On Kulisiewicz's enterprise, see now Makana Eyre, *Sing, Memory: The Remarkable Story of the Man Who Saved the Music of the Nazi Camps*, W. W. Norton & Company, 2023.
19. On music in the camps, see Shirli Gilbert, *Music in the Holocaust*, New York: Oxford University Press, 2005; Roberto Franchini, *L'Ultima nota, Musica I musicisti nei lager nazisti*, Bologna, Marietti , 2021.

remark that his book is not "a book about music," but "about music *in a Nazi concentration camp*," or, alternatively, "about *music in a distorting mirror*."[20] This distinction between "by means of" and "for," which many musicians (and other creators in other fields) experience, is commonplace in ordinary circumstances. It is less so when "living by means of music" means surviving Auschwitz thanks to it.

My father certainly lived "by means of" music for a part of his life. As a violinist before the war he accompanied silent films, played in cafés, and gave lessons. I don't know exactly what year he sailed around the world on a liner as a ship's musician. After the war he composed film music under pseudonyms.[21] He also earned his living in other ways, in particular by working for his brother Leo, who ran a film technology establishment in Saint-Cloud (my father, who knew six languages and more, had also become a specialist in subtitling).[22] But my father also lived for music. In an interview given to the Polish magazine *Ruch Muzyczny* in 1964, he mentioned the extraordinary musical activity of the Young Polish Composers' Society in Paris, founded in 1927, one year after his arrival.[23] The fact that two leading interpreters, Maurice Maréchal and Vlado Perlemuter executed his *Sonata for Cello and Piano* (dedicated to Maurice Maréchal) in 1932 is a sign among others of a growing notoriety which the war was to erase, like that of so many other musicians.

Between the music he wrote after the war over a short period of time and the music "from another world," there is nothing in common.

---

20. *AM*, p.7.
21. Namely Robert Axel and André Lorent. More than 80 titles listed in the catalog of the Society of Authors, Composers and Music Publishers (SACEM).
22. He even left a short handbook, *Le Sous-titrage de films, sa technique, son esthétique*, ownership of the author, published in 1957 (available online in the journal *L'Écran traduit*: http://ataa.fr/revue/)
23. See the interview with T. Kascyński, *Mélodies d'Auschwitz...* (Cerf, 2018), pp. 368ff.

This does not mean that between a life for music, and the experience of the camp, there were not after the war some interferences.

No pre-war work seems to have been marked by the Jewish tradition—my father was clearly one of those assimilated Jews who had broken with religion and tradition, like his two favorite poets, his compatriots Julian Tuwim and Antoni Słonimski.[24] Just after the war, however, he adapted *Eight Jewish Folk Songs*, and, dealing directly with the gas chambers, wrote *Funeral*, with lyrics by Mieczysław Jastrun; later, an *Elegy for Jewish Villages*, based on a famous poem by Słonimski; and a stage music for Perec Hirschbein's *The Blacksmith's Daughters*, a production of the Jewish Theater I remember attending in Paris in 1964 (I was 14 years old). But the presence, after the war, of musical motifs related to the fate of the Jewish people is probably not the most important aspect of the trace left by his encounter with extermination. After returning from the camps, my father composed a few pieces, before practically stopping for a dozen years. The fragility of his health was certainly a factor, as was the need to earn a living. He did not really return to composition until 1962. It was not for long. In 1967, Israel preventively attacked Egypt. Soon after, my father stopped composing. He told me that writing music had lost its meaning for him. I was too young at the time, or too far from his past, to really understand. For him, the war meant that Jewish lives were threatened again. Music was not to survive this shock, which of course does not exclude that other factors may have played a role in his renunciation, notably discouragement, at the end of a career that had never been one.

---

24. Tuwim, the greatest Polish poet of the first half of the 20th century, wrote in 1942 a text, "We Polish Jews," in which my father recognized himself (The text is edited by Ch. Shmeruk in Polish, English, Hebrew and Yiddish, in Julian Tuwim, *My, Żydzi polscy*, Warsaw : Amerykańsko-Polsko-Izraelska Fundacja Shalom, 1993). He wrote several songs based on the words of his poems. It should be noted that Tuwim had written an anti-Semitic poem in the 1930s entitled *Żydzi (The Jews)*. Słonimski had also indulged, in 1930, in dubious statements. My father writes about this bitterly and objectively in *Dziennik pisany w biały dzień* (*Diary written in broad daylight*), London, 1981, pp. 39-44.

Literary activity served as a substitute to some extent. Besides music, my father loved languages and linguistic questions, was interested in translation problems and politics–in particular, in totalitarianism and everything that directly or indirectly concerned Israel. He had a very pronounced taste for sharp polemics, in which he excelled. During the last fifteen years of his life, he translated into French a book by Władysława Jaworska, an art historian and very close friend: *Gauguin and the School of Pont-Aven* (Neuchâtel, 1971); literary texts, mostly related to Jewish matters– the Shoah, for Krystyna Żywulska's *L'Eau vide* (Paris, 1972),[25] Polish anti-Semitism, for Jósef Hen's *L'Œil de Dayan*, published under the pseudonym Korab (Paris, 1974).[26] My father had always maintained a regular correspondence, with friends and, through newspapers, with the Polish emigration, on musical, linguistic and political subjects. At the end of his life he wrote several books in Polish that are built around this correspondence, of which he reproduced some, before destroying most of the rest.[27] The very last books are more like diaries, written day by day. All of them were published, like the Polish version of the book on Auschwitz, by *Oficyna Poetów i Malarzy*. I translate the titles here: *Episodes, Epigrams, Epistles* (1976); *Polonisms, Polemics, Politics* (1977); *Words and Counterwords* (1978); *Profanation of the Holy* (1980); *Diary Written in Broad Daylight* (1981), *The Reduced Fare Costs More* (1982); *My War for Peace* (1983); *Culture with Quotation Marks and Without* (1984). Obviously, he considered that this was, next to music, the legacy he had to leave.

---

25. *Empty water. A memoir of the Warsaw Ghetto* (1963). Concerning the relationship between this book and Krystyna Żywulska's later work on the same subject (*Wo vorher Birken waren. Überlebensbericht einer jungen Frau aus Auschwitz-Birkenau*, Munich, 1979), see his letter to her after its publication (see *Mélodies d'Auschwitz...* , Cerf 2018, p. 339-41).

26. He also translated a few texts by Adolph Rudnicki, which he did not really appreciate. See *Mojna wojna o pokój* (*My War for Peace*), London 1983, pp. 65ss.

27. What was preserved was given by my mother to the Polish Library in Paris (Quai Conti), or is still in my possession.

## ABOUT MY FATHER

My father's musical work was rarely played during his lifetime, and even less in the twenty years following his death, even if his name was not entirely unknown.[28] His rediscovery was first linked to the diffusion of his book and to the question of the role of music in the camps.[29] For a time I have felt upset concerning this state of affairs: My father would certainly have subscribed *mutatis mutandis* to Ruth Klüger's statement: "The name [Auschwitz] has an aura, albeit a negative one, that came with the patina of time, and people who want to say something important about me announce that I have been in Auschwitz. But whatever you may think, I don't hail from Auschwitz, I come from Vienna."[30] This feeling has faded, because I have understood that the question of music in the camps was only one aspect of the broader question of the impact of the politics of totalitarian regimes on the history of twentieth-century music. For the past twenty years many engaged historians and musicologists, publishers and musicians have devoted themselves to the rediscovery, preservation and dissemination of a threatened memory.[31] As far as my father is concerned, the situation has profoundly changed, for the work has begun to be played and appreciated, it now benefits from very good recordings and some works are included in the repertoire

---

28. The great English music encyclopedia, *Grove*, for example, devoted an entry to my father, as did the German encyclopedia *Die Musik in Geschichte und Gegenwart*, Bärenreiter/Metzler, "Personenteil," vol. 7, 2003.

29. My father's name was mentioned, in the thematic section ("Sachteil") of the encyclopedia cited in the previous note, only for his testimony about Auschwitz (article "Theresienstadt," vol. 7, 1997), and not in relationship with the School of Paris, or for his activity in the society of young Polish composers (see vol. 9, 1998). Things have changed. See Frank Harders-Wuthenow's contribution to the present volume and his article (with includes a catalogue of my father's works and discography by Holger Groschopp in Hanns-Werner Heister and Walter-Wolfgang Sparrer (eds,) *Komponisten der Gegenwart* (KDG), Munich: Edition Text.Kritik 2024.

30. Ruth Kluger, *Still alive: a Holocaust girlhood remembered*, New York: Feminist Press at the City University of New York, 2001 (Part 3, Chap. 8).

31. For the consequences of Nazism on the history of music, see Amaury du Closel's *Les Voix étouffées du IIIe Reich*, Actes Sud 2005.

of several ensembles and soloists. It is above all to the determination of Frank Harders-Wuthenow, to whom I cannot express my gratitude enough, that the vast majority of the musical scores are now available through Boosey & Hawkes, Berlin.[32] The text he devotes to my father's music in the present volume shows the extent of his involvement in its rehabilitation.

---

32. The list can be consulted on the site www.boosey.com. The remaining pieces are published in Poland by Polskie Wydawnictwo Muzyczne (PWM).

# Annette Becker
# SIMON LAKS,
# *MUSIC FROM ANOTHER WORLD*

## A Jewish composer in Auschwitz-Birkenau.

"*This is not a book about* music. *It's a book about* music in a Nazi concentration camp," writes Simon Laks in his presentation (*Overture*) of *Auschwitzian Melodies*, written in 1979, that is more than 30 years after *Music From Another World*.[1] Indeed, one of the strength of Laks' testimony in both books lies in the way he recounts his paradoxical undying love of music in a camp of torture and death where Nazis did love music—music of many different kinds—and where music was instrumentalized, making it an object of hatred for the detainees.[2]

In *Music From Another World*, the saxophonist René Coudy, who says "I", describes the other musicians, including Simon Laks, called André in the story he co-signs, and of whom it is sure, from reading the correspondence for the publishing contract and Laks' vain efforts to find Coudy afterwards, that he did more than just co-write it.[3] Through the artifice of the narrative within the narrative, a sort of *mise-en-abyme*, Simon Laks/André comes to say "I", too: He tells the recently arrived Coudy, or rather Khoudy (the spelling of the official document),[4] about his own arrival and his first year at the camp in chapters XII, "Theme and Variations", and XIII "Suites", which are located exactly in the middle of a book that includes 23 musical titles, from "Overture" to "Final Chord." Had the two men been closer intellectually, we might have imagined a relationship such as that which united Pikolo and Primo Levi in Auschwitz and persisted for the rest of their lives, and the choice of "we" to write.[5] But Simon and René lost touch, Simon subsequently wrote alone, and it was his only son born on his return to Paris who inherited—in the strongest sense—the name André.

The precise study of Simon Laks' artistic consciousness allows us, as in a multi-layered musical analysis, to restore historical order to the chaos of the Nazi era. Between May 14, 1941, the date of his arrest in Paris as a foreign Jew, and his return to France on May 24, 1945, Simon Laks survived at least six so-called internment or concentration camps, on French territory and then that of Nazi Germany, which included, at the time of his deportation to the Auschwitz-Birkenau complex in July 1942, the territory of Polish Silesia annexed to the Reich. May 1941 to May 1945: four years, thousands of kilometers traveled by train, bus or truck, hundreds on foot: Paris, the Loiret, Auschwitz-Birkenau, Oranienburg-Sachsenhausen, a stage on the forced evacuation route from Auschwitz, Kaufering (Dachau sub-camp), return to France via Sarreguemines, and finally Paris.[6] Geographical displacements, however, are less vertiginous than the emotional and mental displacements made by the composer, who was born in Warsaw in 1901 and had been leading a very active and recognized life as a composer and performer in Paris since 1926.

## PARIS/PITHIVIERS/AUSCHWITZ-BIRKENAU

*Statute of the Jews*, Vichy, October 4, 1940: "*Article 1*. Foreign nationals of the Jewish race may, from the date of promulgation of the present law, be interned in special camps by decision of the prefect of their place of residence (...) *Article 3*. Foreign nationals of the Jewish race may, at any time, be assigned a forced residence by the prefect of the department of their place of residence."

The day after the promulgation of the *Statute of the Jews*, the French State gave prefects the right to intern "foreign nationals of

Jewish race." While foreigners from belligerent nations had already been interned in France and around the world in concentration camps during the First World War, and again in 1938-39, Vichy policy was an innovation in discrimination. Pétain wanted both to regenerate the France of the "purely French" through work, family and patriotic feelings, and to exclude all those deemed "responsible for the decomposition" of the nation, starting with Jews, deemed to belong to a particular "race." The new xenophobic and, above all, anti-Semitic legislation was a progressive, interconnected enterprise. The denaturalization commission almost only dealt with cases of foreign Jews who had been naturalized since 1927. Six months later, in the spring of 1941, the creation of the Commissariat *Général aux Questions Juives* (General Commissariat for Jewish Questions) enabled the policy of exclusion and persecution to be fine-tuned. It was also intensified under pressure from the German occupation authorities in France: Theodor Dannecker, head of Section IV J of the Gestapo, in charge of the "Jewish question," represented Eichmann.[7] Philippe Pétain's government then used its anti-Jewish legislation and the census of foreign Jews in the Paris region, which had been compiled since September 1940,[8] to have them interned. The decree of October 4, 1940 was French, the internment decision German, the implementation French. In the early days of May 1941, several thousand foreigners and Jews—including Simon Laks—received a green paper summons—hence the name "green ticket round-up"—"inviting" them to "present themselves," on May 14, at various assembly points "for examination of their situation." With their sense of legality and persisting confidence in France, in spite of the ongoing persecution, most of them went along. In this way, 3,700 Jews were arrested, taken to the Gare d'Austerlitz by bus and transferred the same day by train to the Loiret. 1,700 were interned at Pithiviers, 2,000 at Beaune-la-Rolande, including Simon Laks, who remained there until

July, when he was transferred to the Rosoir farm in the Sologne. A year later, on July 13, 1942, he was transferred to the Pithiviers camp, 5 days before his deportation to Auschwitz-Birkenau on July 17 by convoy no. 6.

In May 1941, Simon Laks could not know, no more than any other internee, what was going on in Germany, which was preparing Operation Barbarossa, where the fanatics of the "solution to the Jewish question" were deep in thought. As early as August, advisor Karl Theo Zeitschel, in charge of relations with the General Commissariat for Jewish Questions at the German Embassy in Paris, was hailing German victories in the Soviet Union and the radicalization of the policy of repression against Eastern Jews, who had fallen into the hands of the Nazis in huge numbers—read: mass shootings by the 'Einsatzgruppen.' Zeitschel hoped that a "solution" would also be found for Western Jews. Why not deport them to the East, on a single territory, in particular the Jews of France, given that internment capacity was felt to be insufficient?

Capacities, but also conditions: the camp of Beaune-la-Rolande was designed in 1939 for future German prisoners of war, but when France was defeated, French prisoners were interned there before being transferred to Germany. By 1941, barracks, barbed wire, watchtowers and administration buildings were available. On July 25, Simon Laks volunteered to work on the Rosoir farm in the Sologne, which had been requisitioned by the Loiret prefect. Why this choice of manual farm work? Why distance himself from the other internees and not take part in the camp's activities—particularly musical ones? He may have hoped that the hygiene and food conditions would be better than those in the camp. But these abandoned farms, where collective, superimposed beds had been hastily fitted out to accommodate the internees, were to prove just as inappropriate. Some of them, however, took advantage of the remoteness and sometimes of the complicity of certain farmers to escape; did Laks considered doing so? The internees hardly ever saw Germans, except on the occasion of a few inspection visits, such as that of Dannecker at Pithiviers, who had the nerve to declare in June 1941 that the conditions of internment were not up to standard, and criticized the French authorities for their poor management. The internees would only meet up with the Germans again, alongside the French gendarmes, when they boarded the cattle cars heading east.

Simon Laks was part of convoy no. 6, which left directly from Pithiviers on July 17, 1942, without passing through Drancy. What did he know, what did he think? The last letters from two deportees on the same convoy are likely to reflect common feelings. Already the vague idea of death, quickly erased, to reassure their loved ones; for in the summer of 1942, the facts are already known: "We are leaving today for the East and not for the Sologne as we were initially told. So I'm leaving today. Perhaps we'll meet again in Poland. Don't worry, darling. They won't kill so many people. (...) I've come to tell you that I'm leaving today evening. I think we're going to work."[9] Meanwhile, in Paris, the Vel d'Hiv roundup had been going on since July 16th, and space had to be made in Pithiviers and Beaune-la-Rolande for the newly arrested. In the morning, a telex was sent by the anti-Jewish section of the Paris Gestapo to Eichmann in Berlin, to the Camp Inspectorate in Oranienburg and to the commandant of Auschwitz. At 06:15 a.m., "*Laks Szymon, 01.11.01 Warsaw,*" was deported with 927 other Jews, including 119 women and some children, the youngest being 12 years old. On arrival on July 19, the 809 men and teenagers were given the serial numbers 48880 to 49688, the 119 women 9550 to 9968. Simon Laks is now 49543. He was selected to enter and be registered at the camp in terror, dereliction and incomprehension, the majority of the others were exterminated immediately.[10]

*"THE ONLY REALITY OF THIS SEVENTY-TWO-HOUR TRIP WAS THE UNIMAGINABLE CRUSH OF DEPORTEES IN CATTLE CARS AND THE HALLUCINATIONS CAUSED BY A THIRST THAT WAS IMPOSSIBLE TO QUENCH."*

"*Hallucinations*": wasn't it one of them to have spotted the sign for an exceptional town while passing through a railway station? "*Johann Sebastian Bach was born in Eisenach on March 21, 1685. Such was my first encounter with music during my deportation.*"[11]

In the world before, there were Bach and Beethoven, German musicians; in the world of Auschwitz-Birkenau, they were still there, but could one talk and perhaps above all hear them, in the counter-world where he has been thrown?[12] His exceptional analyses restitute with great acuity, in every sense of the word, the "musical" violence of the camp : the music we make, the music we are forced to make, or worse, to hear. Sounds, screams, blows, musical notes, more screams and blows, concerts and death.

July 19, 1942: background sounds: "*Guttural yelling od the floggers and the long-drawn out moans of the flogged. Athletes in stripes belaboring us with cudgels, yelling for the very pleasure of yelling: Los! Aufstehen! Raus! Aber schnell!*"[13] We're no longer in Poland, in Oświęcim, but in Auschwitz, Reich territory, where the language—the scream—is German.

How is it possible to make the world after Auschwitz, hear and understand what Auschwitz, the implacable reversal of all human reality, was like? Witold Pilecki, a Pole who voluntarily entered the Auschwitz camp to organize the resistance in 1940, testified in 1945 to the atrocious brutality of the arrival of his convoy, the murder of ten of them, the dogs let loose excited by blood: "I had the impression of leaving Earth, of entering another world. (...) All our ideas, our concepts about life, society on earth, the law, all that was also brutally collapsing."[14] Simon Laks describes this zone of lawlessness and non-humanity well: *"This collision with camp life had plunged me into a lethargic stupor and at the same time as though I had been shot from a catapult to another planet. (...) What kind of world is this? (...) I tried to shake off this nightmare, tell myself that it was a dream, but the awakening did not come."*[15]

Simon Laks arrived at Auschwitz in 1942, "the most monstrous year", says Pilecki: the concentration and forced-labor camp was now joined by an extermination site, Birkenau. These are twins, or rather Siamese twins: they live through each other, with initial selection feeding both parts by successfully bringing together the three sides of the system: forced labor, dehumanization, and extermination. The first convoys of Jews arrived at Birkenau on March 26 and 27, from Poprad (Slovakia) and the Bourget-Drancy railway station, the first convoy to come from France. In 1940, Auschwitz had become the 7th concentration camp on Reich territory; in 1942, Birkenau became the 6th Jewish extermination center after Chelmno, Belzec, Sobibor, Treblinka and Majdanek, all located within the Polish protectorate. Auschwitz-Birkenau was the place where most Jews—and Gypsies—were killed, and where most Poles and Soviet prisoners died either by exhaustion or by execution.

On July 17 and 18, the exact days of Simon Laks' "great journey,"[16] Himmler came to Birkenau to witness the "processing" of a convoy from the Netherlands, a convincing demonstration of the efficiency of the technical "platform": sorting of around 20% of the human raw material for forced labor, registration and tattooing, gassing of 80% of the arrivals, evacuation of the corpses by the members of the *Sonderkommando*, then recovering of clothes, women's hair, gold teeth, prostheses, burning of the rest in the crematoriums, evacuation of the ashes. Himmler, "Reich Commissioner for the Strengthening of the German Nation" appreciated this extraordinary "modern migration of population" this "removal of human ballast," this "ethnic cleansing," as he put it: the hoped for radicalization had finally led to the elimination of undesirable "waste": German purity would be guaranteed.

The entire Nazi war economy had become dependent on the work of prisoners of war, conscript laborers and internees in the concentration camps and their thousands of *Kommandos*. Reich Minister of Justice Otto Georg Thierack spoke of an "extermination through labor."[17] Indeed, work is not antithetical to the extermination of the Jews, but rather a phase of the process, one of the components of the industrial organization of mass murder.

## *"IF YOU ARE ACCEPTED IN THE ORCHESTRA, YOU HAVE A CHANCE TO GET OUT."*[18]

Why, then, exhaust the prisoners selected for labor by starvation and beatings, kill large numbers of them just to satisfy the sadism of certain executioners, when there was a real need for this labor force? Jacques Sémelin coined the oxymoron of "delusional rationality,"[19] which Simon Laks conveyed perfectly. The day after his arrival, caught up in the cries of the call, he was taken aback: *"I then see, in the alley, a few men loaded with wooden objects whose shape seems familiar. The idea seems so absurd (…) Could it be a mirage? (…) They're music stands, music stands! (…) vestige of logic (…) Let us reason. Where there are music stands there are musicians (…) So who plays music here? The executioners or the victims? What is the of music that resounds in this cursed place? Macabre dances? Funeral marches? Hitlerian songs?"*[20]

Yes, music resounds in the madness of these places, at Auschwitz first of all, ordered by the camp commandant, Rudolf Höss, from January 1941 onwards. The Birkenau orchestra was founded in the summer of 1942, initially with musicians from Auschwitz 1, Poles like Ludwik Żuk, who became its conductor and was instrumental in recruiting Laks, one of the first Jews to join the orchestra. There were also orchestras in Monowitz, Golleschau and Blechhamer, and a women's ensemble in Birkenau, which sometimes played with the men's, a manifestation of "*cultural exchanges.*"[21] Piotr Rawicz testifies: "Any self-respecting camp commander had to have an orchestra, just as he had to have a brothel, just as a modern city wants to have its opera house. This caricature of reality, this sort of decor, this sham, belonged to the system."[22]

Höss, who had acquired excellent professional credentials in Dachau and Sachsenhausen, had also borrowed the inscription "*Arbeit Macht Frei,*" which had been circulating in *völkisch* circles since the 19th century. Musicians were thus, like all other inmates, enrolled in the camp's main endeavor: working oneself to death. For them, this is at the second degree, since the function of the music *Kommando* is to punctuate the departure and return from work: so that the slaves leave the camp or return from their *Kommandos* more quickly and are thus more easily counted and recounted, the Nazis' obsession being to always have a perfect headcount, dead or alive. "*No, we didn't play funeral marches. On the contrary, the marches we played (...) were gay, lively, joyous, varied, and their role was to encourage work and the joy of life in the name of the camp slogan* Arbeit Macht Frei *(Work makes man free).*"[23] Primo Levi recounted his surprise on the first evening, when still in quarantine, in February 1944, he saw the forced laborers returning: "A band begins to play, next to the entrance of the camp: it plays *Rosamunda*, the well known sentimental song, and this seems so strange to us that we look sniggering at each other (...) the band, on finishing *Rosamunda*, continues to play other marches, one after the other, and suddenly the squads of our comrades appear, returning from work. They walk in columns of five with a strange, unnatural hard gait, like stiff puppets made of jointless bones; but they walk scrupulously in time to the band."[24] Later, Levi adds: "The tunes are few, a dozen, the same ones every day, morning and evening: marches and popular songs dear to every German. They lie engraven on our minds and will be the last thing in *Lager* that we shall forget: they are the voice of the *Lager*, the perceptible expression of its geometrical madness, of the resolution of others to annihilate us first as men in order to kill us more slowly afterwards. When this music plays we know that our comrades, out in the fog, are marching like automatons; their souls are dead and the music drives them, like the wind drives dead leaves, and takes the place of their wills (…) At the departure and the return march the SS are never lacking. Who could deny them their right to watch this choreography of their creation, the dance of dead men, squad after squad, leaving the fog to enter the fog? What more concrete proof of their victory?"[25]

Primo Levi understood that music in the camp was a kind of torture for those who were forced to listen to it—himself in this case—as well as for those who were obliged to perform it,[26] but also that it belonged to the "miracle" of survival, like chemistry for him. Unwilling musicians are spared not only because they participate in the valorization of other prisoners' work, but also because they make it possible. Simon Laks insists: *"We are all a small but concrete part of the formidable German war machine. Because the German cannot imagine anything without music, ours is also a substantial cog in this machine."*[27]

Finally, the *Lagerkappelle* can sometimes have something artistic or solemn when musicians play on Sundays for the SS and during visits of dignitaries; in this case it makes the difficult life of the SS more pleasant; thanks to their "love of music," they command better and are more attentive to the efficacy of their cruel and deadly tasks.

## "THE VIOLIN I AM HOLDING HAS BECOME MY SHIELD."

In the summer of 1942, Birkenau and its orchestra were just getting up and running. Simon was not immediately spotted, and owes it to one of the many *"miracles"* of survival that he finally joined the music *Kommando*. This happened in two stages: he began by playing from time to time, while continuing to slave away at other tasks, mainly carting stones. Some *Kapos* need a Polish-speaking bridge player: "*That evening, their usual 'fourth' for bridge was busy welcoming new victims to his block, and to this that I owed the honorable role that had befallen me: that of worthy partner to a man who tomorrow might turn out to be my executioner. Fate had it that my potential murderer became my savior.*" The card players discover that he can also do well as a musician: "*Why didn't you tell me sooner? Tomorrow you'll stay in the barracks and I'll take you over to the orchestra (...) And if you're accepted, may be you'll live a little longer (...) My block leader is proving to be a man of his word. When he has to kill, he kills; when he helps, he helps to the very end.*"[28] Dressed in a special uniform and carrying a violin, Laks put a second space between himself and death, after that of selection on arrival. "*This violin I am hold has become my shield.*"[29] But as long as he continues to go out as an ordinary labor *Kommando*, the *Himmelkommando* ("The *Kommando* of the sky") is still waiting for him.

The second phase is that of an almost definitive rescue—as far as we can use such a term when any *kapo* or SS officer can kill you at any moment—due to the torturers' desire for music. When Simon Laks' superior musical skills were spotted, he became a music copyist, *Notenschreiber*, and later a conductor, *Kappelmeister*.

René Khoudy, for his part, was arrested in Paris on July 6, 1943, interned at Drancy from July 7 to 17, and deported to the Birkenau camp on convoy no. 57 on July 18, 1943. Two firsts for this train carrying 1126 human beings, from old people to infants: it left from the Drancy-Bobigny station, and the usual telex to Eichmann and the Auschwitz camp was signed by Aloïs Brunner, commandant of Drancy since June 18. Khoudy, born in 1908, aged 35, was one of the 369 men and 191 women registered, no. 130651. The 566 others were gassed immediately, including his father, Jacob, and his mother, Berthe Bechlebicky, who were deported with him. In 1945, 43 survived, including René Khoudy.

Having "entered" the Birkenau camp in 1943, a year after Simon Laks—a geological era in this context—Coudy (the name was Frenchized for the book of 48, like Szymon's first name already before the war) benefited from the advice of the "elders." Khoudy, who plays the saxophone as an amateur, joins the *Lagerkapelle*, where he finds a Simon Laks (noted as *Musiker*, musician), or *Komponist, composer*, on the camp lists) now at the head of some forty musicians. Being part of this ensemble means that they no longer have to work outside the camp, they get enough to eat, stay in a decent barrack corner and meet deported Polish musicians who started out in the Auschwitz 1 orchestra.

As a professional, Simon Laks wonders about music in such a place, and about instruments: *"Music is a luxury item, and as such, an essentially 'organizable' material."*[30] *"Music is an article of consumption par excellence and as such was subject to the skill of organizing. (...) With the continually increasing influx of 'gas meat' and the accompanying prosperity of the privileged classes of Auschwitz society, this industry took on the dimensions of hitherto unknown luxury."*[31] This "luxury" concerns the musicians themselves, their instruments, the scores. As for the men capable of repairing the instruments that arrive in their hands in more or less lamentable condition, just like the musicians capable of playing them, they are as indispensable.

**COMITÉ INTERNATIONAL DE LA CROIX-ROUGE**
SERVICE INTERNATIONAL DE RECHERCHES
Arolsen (Waldeck) Allemagne
INTERNATIONAL TRACING SERVICE — INTERNATIONALER SUCHDIENST
Arolsen (Waldeck) Germany — Arolsen (Waldeck) Deutschland

No. 78250

Certificate of Incarceration — Inhaftierungsbescheinigung — Certificat d'Incarcération

Our Ref.: TD 670362

| | | |
|---|---|---|
| Name: KHOUDY | First names: René | Nationality: französisch |
| Date of birth: 24.9.1908 | Place of birth: Paris | Prisoner's No.: 130651 im KL.Auschwitz |
| Parents' names: Jacob u. Berthe BESCHLEBICKY | | |

It is hereby certified that the following information is available in documentary evidence held by the International Tracing Service.

Name: KHOUDY — First names: René — Nationality: französisch
Date of birth: 24.9.1908 — Place of birth: Paris — Profession: Schneider, Elektriker-
Parents' names: Jacob u. Berthe geb. BESCHLIBICKY, (beide im KL.Auschwitz gestorben)
Last permanent residence: Paris, rue Richer 20 oder Paris, 40, Bvd.Bonne Nouvelle..
entered concentration camp: Sammellager Drancy — Prisoner's No.: nicht angeführt----
on: nicht angeführt----- coming from: nicht angeführt--------------------------------
Category, or reason given for incarceration: "Sch." (Schutzhaft) "Jude"----------------
Transferred: am 18/20.Juli 1943 zum KL.Auschwitz, Häftl.Nr.: 130651. Überstellung nicht angeführt. Er wurde am 17.November 1944 vom KL.Sachsenhausen in das KL.Dachau eingeliefert, Häftl.Nr. 127354 und zum KL.Dachau/Kdo.Kaufering überstellt (Datum nicht angeführt)..........................................
Liberated: durch die US-Army -------- in KL.Dachau/Kdo. Kaufering.----------------
Remarks: In den Häftlingspersonalbogen ist vermerkt: "Verhaftet am: 6.7.43" bezw. "7.7.43 wo:Paris". "Einweisende Dienststelle: RSHA" und im Häftlingspersonalbogen des KL.Auschwitz ist ausser der Auschwitz-Häftlingsnummer noch die Nr. 111119 angeführt.-----------------------------------
Über den Aufenthalt nach dem 8.Mai 1945 liegen keine Unterlagen vor.----------
Documents consulted: Transportlisten des Sammellagers Drancy, Häftlingspersonalbogen des KL.Auschwitz, Schreibstubenkarte, Häftlingspersonalbogen und Zugangsbuch des KL.Dachau.--------------------------------------

Arolsen,

**AKTENKOPIE**
**Formblattänderung**

Directeur
Service International de Recherches

Section des Archives

Pl. Gr.
MR.

Der ITS übernimmt für die Richtigkeit und Vollständigkeit des Inhalts der Dokumente, die zur Ausstellung dieser Bescheinigung verwendet wurden, keine Gewähr.

* Erklärung des I.S.D., erscheint nicht in den Originalunterlagen.
* Explication fournie par le S.I.R., mais ne figurant pas sur les documents originaux.
* Added by the I.T.S. as explanation, does not appear on the original documents.

Bitte wenden!

After the war, the International Committee of the Red Cross (ICRC) was given the task of compiling all the data on the camps...

**COMITÉ INTERNATIONAL DE LA CROIX-ROUGE**
SERVICE INTERNATIONAL DE RECHERCHES
Arolsen (Waldeck) Allemagne
INTERNATIONAL TRACING SERVICE    INTERNATIONALER SUCHDIENST
Arolsen (Waldeck) Germany    Arolsen (Waldeck) Deutschland

No. 66380

Certificate of Incarceration    Inhaftierungsbescheinigung    Certificat d'Incarcération

| | | |
|---|---|---|
| Ihr Akt.-Z.: Votre Réf.: Your Ref.: | Reg.Präs.Köln; (Intr. RA.Tauchner, MÜ) | Unser Akt.-Z.: Notre Réf.: Our Ref.: T/D 502 320 |
| Name / Nom / Name | LAKS | Vornamen / Prénoms / First names: Simon — Staatsangehörigkeit / Nationalité / Nationality: polnisch |
| Geburtsdatum / Date de naissance / Date of birth | 1.11.1901 | Geburtsort / Lieu de naissance / Place of birth: Warschau — Häftlingsnummer / No. de prisonnier / Prisoner's No.: -49543- im KL. Auschwitz |
| Name der Eltern / Noms des parents / Parents' names | Isaac und Sarah Hellemer | |

It is hereby certified that the following information is available in documentary evidence held by the International Tracing Service. / Es wird hiermit bestätigt, daß folgende Angaben in den Unterlagen des Internationalen Suchdienstes aufgeführt sind. / Il est certifié par la présente que les informations suivantes se trouvent dans la documentation détenue par le Service International de Recherches.

| | | |
|---|---|---|
| Name | LAKS | Vornamen: Simon — Staatsangehörigkeit: französisch |
| Geburtsdatum | 1.11.1901 | Geburtsort: Warschau — Beruf: Musiker |
| Name der Eltern | Isaak und Sara Hellemer | |

Zuletzt bekannter ständiger Wohnsitz / Dernière adresse connue / Last permanent residence: Paris 38 rue Boulard

wurde eingeliefert in das Lager / est entré au camp / has entered: Sammellager Beaune-la-Rolande — Häftlingsnummer: nicht angeführt

am / le / on: nicht angeführt — von / venant de / coming from: nicht angeführt

Kategorie, oder Grund für die Inhaftierung / Catégorie, ou raison donnée pour l'incarcération / Category, or reason given for incarceration: " Sch." (Schutzhaft) " Jude "

Überstellt / Transféré / Transferred: am 17. Juli 1942 zum KL. Auschwitz. Er wurde am 17.November 1944 vom KL. Sachsenhausen in das KL. Dachau eingeliefert, Häftl.Nr. 126924; zum KL. Dachau/Kdo. Kaufering überstellt (Datum nicht angeführt.

Befreit / Libéré / Liberated: durch die "US-" Army"    im / en / in: KL. Dachau/Kdo.Kaufering

Bemerkungen / Remarques / Remarks: Im Häftlingspersonalbogen ist vermerkt:"Verhaftet am: 14.1.1941 wo: Paris." -- Abweichung: "Staatsangehörigkeit:"französisch" ---------- Krankenpapiere liegen nicht vor.

Geprüfte Unterlagen / Documents consultés / Records consulted: Transportliste des Sammellagers Beaune-la-Rolande; Zugangsbuch, Schreibstubenkarte und Häftlingspersonalbogen des KL. Dachau.

Arolsen, den 7. Dezember 1956

A. DE COCATRIX
Directeur adjoint
Service International de Recherche

A. OPITZ
Section des Archives

Er. Hu.
St.Dir.

Der ITS übernimmt für die Richtigkeit und Vollständigkeit des Inhalts der Dokumente, die zur Ausstellung dieser Bescheinigung verwendet wurden, keine Gewähr.

* Erklärung des I.S.D., erscheint nicht in den Originalunterlagen.
* Explication fournie par le S.I.R. mais ne figurant pas sur les documents originaux.
* Added by the I.T.S. as explanation, does not appear on the original documents.

(bitte wenden)

...which was then gathered at Arolsen in Germany into a gigantic archive that was consulted by survivors, who sometimes found in it the only trace of their loved ones - a name on a card.

## A JEWISH COMPOSER IN AUSCHWITZ-BIRKENAU.

## MUSIC AND EXTERMINATION

Initially housed in block 15, the musicians, their instruments and scores moved to block 5, where they were already sleeping. The *Musikstube*, where those who were no longer working outside during the day and where rehearsals took place, was heated, a luxury the instruments needed and which the musicians took advantage of. Simon Laks is overwhelmed by what he discovers there on his recruitment: "*My attention was first attracted, 'professionally' one might say, by the wooden partition a few meters away on which were hanging all sorts of brass and woodwind instruments, everything polished to a bright shine. I distinguished in turn a huge tuba helicon, a trombone, a few trumpets, a brass tenor and alto horns, saxophones, clarinets and two flutes, one a piccolo. Leaning against the wall in one of the corners, was an impressive double bass with a bow stuck under the strings, in another a bass drum with cymbals with all of the percussion paraphernalia. On a wide, solid shelf specifically designated for this purpose were a few accordions and violins in cases. One of them, somewhat bigger than the others, probably contained a viola. I failed to see a cello. A second shelf, somewhat smaller, was filled with music scores and a pile of blank music paper.*"[32] The musician takes such pleasure in making an inventory of instruments that he returns to it very often, as when he describes the orchestra taking their places for the marches intended to punctuate the departure and return from forced labor, as if the names of the violins, tubas, horns, etc. could magically take him back to his life, his life before.[33] But he never forgets, even during the description of the music barrack and the brass band, that he is still in the camp. He seems to lengthen his precise enumeration of instruments into a veritable litany to make the time of the "mirage" last; for, as he rehearses, he never ceases to see cement poles, electrified barbed wire, the undead at work on the other side of the window, and even an SS man who stops to listen to him play.

Being part of the music at Birkenau also rhymes with "organization" and contradictions. Indeed, everything can be called into question, from one moment to the next, by mortal blows or selection for the gas chamber. The only, but extraordinary, prerogative of musicians, as of all "*Prominente*" is a certain life expectancy. But the price they sometimes had to pay was to be seen by other inmates as collaborators of the Nazis. As if they had any choice between dying and playing music, since in Birkenau, everything took place against a backdrop of gas chambers....[34] Contrary to other witnesses,[35] Simon Laks denies, in his distinctive sarcastic tone, any involvement of music in the hanging of prisoners: "*I am not absolving the orchestra, I am absolving the Germans, who love music too much to use it for such prosaic purposes.*"[36] One could argue that punctuating the departures of *Kommandos* to work and their returns was a most "prosaic" purpose, too. In fact, the military fanfare-style playing helped with the counting, to the rhythm, of the exhausted men lined up in rows of five. This is no doubt why, in some cases, inmates insulted the musicians and threw mud at them, and why Michel Borwicz denies having listened to the music at the Janov camp: "We didn't listen to this orchestra, it was one of the elements in the machinery."[37] A Polish inmate from the Birkenau women's camp concurs: "*the procession passes to the rhythm of a light marching melody; shadows of human beings trail along, bending under the weight of the corpses of their companions in misery. How we hated music.*"[38]

Simon Laks never forgets that, from 1942 onwards, Birkenau was first and foremost Europe's largest center for the extermination of Jews, even if music had no direct role in it ... except "incidentally", as is so excruciatingly reported in the chapter "*Directed cacophony.*" "*It is not entirely true that music (...) was intended to officially accompany manifestations of horror, such as the transportation of victims to the gas chambers, shootings, hangings, public beatings, etc. This was the effect of chance and a lack of administrative correlation of these two branches of activity.*" One Sunday, for example, when the musicians were playing in the open air for the SS and inmates, one of the flutists, a doctor from Toulouse, "*is just playing a large-scale solo in which he puts all his energy (…) He is so absorbed in his playing that he does not see the pattern of the trucks loaded with naked women passing on the road and heading towards the crematorium. The trucks disappeared around the bend. In one of them was the daughter of our flutist.*"[39]

Laks, who has become the orchestra's conductor, tries to save his musicians by making their parts indispensable, but he also has a trick, consisting in adding important themes on various scores so that surviving musicians can always replace their murdered colleagues. Black humor from the man who calls himself a "*musical mortician*"[40] Later, Laks even succeeded in having his musicians exempted from further kommando work by pointing to the necessity of protecting their fingers, their scores and their instruments by heavy weather, rain or snow. "*The rain becomes heavier and soaks our scores, blurring the notes written in ink. Kopka* (the Polish Kapo who became the orchestra's first-time conductor) *signals to the violins to put away their instruments and pick up the music notebooks. (…) The drums are still playing their two spaced blows, three close blows. (…) I am soaked to the bone (…) Most of the musicians are struggling with their flooded instruments. Only the brass and the cymbals save the situation and hold on, as best they can, until the end.*"[41] The astute Laks does not argue that the musicians are fragile, but rather that the instruments themselves are "*difficult to contradict, especially for a German who loves music: the instruments were in danger of deteriorating.*"[42]

*"THE INMATES ARE NOW LIVING BETTER AND BETTER, AND THIS IMPROVEMENT IS CORRELATED WITH THE EVER-INCREASING FLOW OF THOSE WHO, COMING FROM OUTSIDE, ARE DIRECTED TO THE CREMATORIUM WITHOUT RECEIVING ANY NUMBER."* [43]

The extortion of personal belongings from camp arrivals took place in three stages, in three places. First, the arrival dock, where various items of luggage were piled up. "*These disparate parcels form a heap sometimes reaching the heights of a building: a real gigantic still life.*"[44] Then it's on to *Canada*, where everything is sorted, and finally the *Effektenlager* or "effects camp", where what's to be sent directly to Germany is stored. At each stage, the musicians try to salvage—to "organize"—what they need, not only for their musical activity—instruments and scores—but also anything that can improve their lives. In the camp where life is played out as at a "*stock market,*"[45] the lot of the musicians is among the most enviable. The rehearsal barracks were used for a variety of salvaging and remunerative activities: watchmaking, language courses, carpentry, theft—tobacco, food, medicine, clothing. The scene is that of an continuous transfer of skills and services, right up to the private concerts performed for the Kapos or SS, "the audience of choice", as Laks ironically puts it in Chapter XV ("The Symphony of Chaos").

This "organization" enabled the musicians to constantly improve their accommodation, their food and their musical lives: "*We now have a large and attractive room, with special facilities for instruments and for writing (…) In this room, a dozen or so musicians and their pupils can be accommodated. When circumstances permit, chamber music sessions are held here in the evening, in the presence of a select audience.*"[46] Depending on the moment, they can "organize" a piano or a double bass in order to improve the orchestra's sound. They repair instruments, either for themselves or in the service of some SS. Portrait of Heinz Lewin, "*a remarkable musician as well as luthier and clockmaker (...)* Heinz "*is absorbed in the reconstruction of an accordion found in pieces in who knows where. He is said to be able to restore any damaged musical instrument.*"[47] This is why *SS Rottenführer* Broad, "*the best friend of our music*", entrusts him with his magnificent personal accordion that he wishes to improve further: "*For several weeks he remained at work on Broad's accordion, hand-cutting all the parts needed to make the small levers and gears that operate this precision mechanism.*"[48] The reward: 250 cigarettes.

*Canada* is the heart of all trafficking. "*All of this, added to the 'merchandise' coming from the despoiling of hundreds of thousands of people sent directly to the gas chambers, ended up generating a prodigious economic world, with its privileged and proletarian classes, with its prices, with its fluctuations, with a stock market.*"[49] The objects of Canada sketch the portrait of human beings who have been caught up in the death machine: "*pile of various objects that seem to be destined for the waste. Among these miscellaneous objects, one can distinguish: glasses, prayer books, children's dolls, photographs, passports, walking sticks, umbrellas....*"[50] And musical instruments. Behind this motley inventory, individuals. For it is not objects that have been "discarded", but human beings; this pair of glasses, this doll, this instrument is unique, a given photograph, even more so, belonged to a unique human being, now murdered and surviving through these unique items. Accumulation does much more than describe: it brings the murdered back to life: "*ten meters away, on the other side of the barbed-wire fence, stand the rectangular chimneys of the crematoriums that burn, burn without ceasing, the owners of the luggage (...).*"[51]

The orchestra's recovery of instruments from the Czech families' camp, then from that of the Gypsy families after their total extermination, is highly representative of the whole system of chanelling the remains. The 4,000 Czech Jewish deportees who arrived from Terezin in the autumn of 1943 enjoy at first a privileged status. They "*live (...) in families. They keep their hair, their personal clothing, and receive letters and packages. In addition, they do not work. Their privileged treatment is an enigma for us and never ceases to arouse our envy.*"[52] The Machiavellian idea was to get the Czechs to write to those still in Terezin about the very relatively livable conditions they had experienced in Birkenau, and so to use them in the enterprise of concealing the extermination to the International Red Cross.[53] But in March 1944, "*atrocious news (...) the Czechs were exterminated by gas, in one night, after six months of a comfortable life of which we were jealous.*"[54] The orchestra, whose equipment was known to be in poor condition, was offered the chance to recover its music stands and instruments. Laks is well aware that it is thanks to this "organization" that he survives through music, and does better and better from 1942 to 1945.

On the night of August 2 to 3, 1944, the *Zigeunernacht*, the camp for Gypsy families was liquidated. Members of the camp's orchestra had been familiar with the Gypsies since the spring of 1943 because of common involvement in various traffics linked to Canada's activities. The two groups had spotted each other's musicians and instruments, and had even "organized" (once again in the double sense of the word) joint concerts. Coincidence? Laks links the decision to do away with Gypsies to one of these concerts, when, panicked by the arrival of Mengele, "*who supervises the human merchandise unloaded at Auschwitz,*" the musicians urge a certain "*Bobby, who has some irresistibly funny numbers in his repertoire (...) to perform to cheer up our distinguished listener. And the miracle happens. In the face of our entertainer's boisterous whimsy, Mengele held back a laugh with his hand, and, as if thwarted by his lack of willpower, suddenly left without uttering a word.*"⁵⁵ Laks recalls that the next day the Gypsies are kidnapped and murdered, and the musicians have to clear their deserted camp... and so can recover some of their instruments, guitars and violins, for the orchestra. The "miracle" has not saved the Gypsies, quite the contrary, but has benefited the "official" musicians.

One day, Major Schwarzhuber's two "blond children" came to attend one of the "official" Sunday concerts: *"He probably has to explain to them how the evil enemies of the beloved Führer are punished and chastised. On the other hand, he must be careful not to tell them where the smoke that blackens the sky comes from. (...) Nor does he tell them that SS Mohl, in charge of the crematoria, is having fun with other small children, grabbing them by the legs to smash their little heads against a wall (...) Lagerführer Schwarzhuber orders us to play 'Heimat deine Sterne'."*⁵⁶ Is this ironic, too? *Heimat*, the native fatherland, suggests the nostalgia lodged in the heart of every German: a nostalgia for purity that could be fulfilled in the apocalyptic fury of the camps and the extermination. Schwarzhuber, who became commandant of the subcamps at Kaufering—where, coincidentally, S. Laks and R. Khoudy were evacuated in 1945—and then at Ravensbrück, took charge, with a small commando led by Mohl, of executing prisoners too weak to leave the camp during forced evacuations.

## FROM AUSCHWITZ TO OTHER CAMPS

As the Soviets were advancing towards Auschwitz-Birkenau, the Nazis decided to evacuate this immense complex of camps in Upper Silesia, in the middle of winter. The members of the orchestra left the Auschwitz station in cattle cars, rather than on foot—another exorbitant privilege. After a stopover at Oranienburg-Sachsenhausen, the musicians were dispersed to various camps further west: for Laks and Khoudy, Dachau and its sub-camp no. 11, Kaufering, where

Simon Laks worked in a gigantic underground aircraft factory.

On May 3, 1945, the Americans freed him by offering him a pack of cigarettes: "*Hitler's dead. How're you? OK.*" Simon Laks returned to Paris on May 18—not without difficulty; in Sarreguemines he had to "*...prove to the French authorities that I was really me.*" He goes to the movies; on the news, American troops blow up an underground factory in Kaufering: "*This was 'my' factory! (...) My last stage! I felt a little strange. So much work for nothing.*"[57] Given the horror of the forced evacuations, known as the death marches,[58] and the abominable conditions described by the Americans when they liberated Kaufering, one wonders why Simon Laks doesn't dwell on the aftermath of Auschwitz, any more than he did on the Loiret camps before. Is it not that Auschwitz-Birkenau was "his" camp, the one where he had practiced his profession as a musician, the one where, as a Jew, he should have been exterminated?

## WITNESSING, BUT HOW?

Simon Laks believed that he has to survive in order to bear witness, hence his early decision not to "*go to the wires*" to commit suicide: "*I wanted to see everything, to experience everything, to learn everything, to record everything. (...) Simply because I did not want to count myself out, to eliminate the witness I could be.*"[59]

Paradoxically, it is through the case of SS Joachim Wolff, emblematic of the schizophrenia of the SS, that Simon Laks makes clear what is at stake there. Wolff, who loves music to the point of becoming close to some musicians of the orchestra, was well aware by the autumn of 1944 that the war was lost, but remained convinced that nobody would ever know about the extermination camps: everything would be done to ensure that there would be no witnesses. But there was more to it: "*Even if there are witnesses and they speak out,* no one will believe them. *This is the genius of our Führer (...).*"[60]

Wolff shares, thanks to his faith in "*the genius of our Führer*", the bitter certainties of certain victims, well identified for example by Aharon Appelfeld:

"*One night, I heard one of the refugees say: 'There are horrors about which it is forbidden to speak.*

*—Another refugee wondered, "Why?*

*—I can't explain.*

*—We're obliged to tell everything, so that everyone knows what's been done to us.*

*—I'm not going to argue with you.*

*—If we're not witnesses, who will be?*

*—We won't be believed anyway.*"[61]

Witness in such a way that the world can "believe". This is what Simon Laks decides to do as early as 1945, finding, and not finding, Paul Celan's famous verses:

"No one
testifies for
the witness."[62]

SS Wolff expressed another idea about secrecy and judgment, and history has not proved him wrong: "*Even if we lose the war, we will not be presented with a 'bill'. Your judgment, if there is one, will be made in a public court, in broad daylight, on the basis of a penal code that will no longer be equal to the 'offenses' committed. Your judges will then be led to declare themselves incompetent. No 'humane' justice can punish arbitrariness with arbitrariness. At most, the great leaders will have to justify themselves. But Germany will always live.*"[63] In 1945, the "great leaders" were tried at Nuremberg, followed by second-rank leaders; for Auschwitz, the 1947 trial in Poland was followed by the Frankfurt trial in the early 1960s; other "great leaders" were found and tried, the case of Eichmann tried in Israel in 1962 being the most emblematic. But the second and third knives of the extermination, such as Joachim Wolff, were forgotten until the 80s, 90s or 2000s, when those who were still alive, now very old, were sometimes caught up in their crimes. Who could then "testify for the witness" and in particular for the "witness" without testimony, the one who was exterminated just as he was about to face the reality of the camps? Who had the right to speak as Simon Laks, talking about the evacuation of the camp, did in 1979, with the moral delicacy that is his trademark : *"With misty eyes I looked at our beautiful Musikstube, said farewell to the instruments arranged in perfect order, to the pile of filled-in music paper, to the table at which I had sat safely for so many days, weeks, months. It is shameful to admit it, but I left Birkenau with regret."*[64] This may not have been sayable in 1948, but was it any more so in 1979?

## WRITING JUST AFTER BIRKENAU

In November 1947, the *Grand Prix Vérité* was created by the daily *Le Parisien libéré* to reward a true story or reportage. Pierre Nord, the first winner, recounts in *Mes camarades sont morts* (*My companions are dead*) the story of the resistance networks in which the intelligence professional and writer of spy novels had participated. This literary prize, the logical consequence of the times, rewards the French Resistance.

However, the manuscript of *Musiques d'un autre monde* also reached the jury, whose president is none other than the still all-powerful—he has resigned—perpetual secretary of the Académie française, Georges Duhamel. He makes it that an "exceptional distinction" be awarded to the manuscript[65] and, above all, proposes to quickly publish it in the *Mercure de France*.[66] In a way, he balanced the reward offered to the Resistance with a mention of the persecuted Jews he had been interested in since before the war. What's more, he acknowledges the specific nature of deportation to Auschwitz, which was extremely rare at the time.[67] Simon Laks, who wrote all the letters on behalf of the two authors, then asked Duhamel for "the great honor of prefacing" their work, and the book was published in January 1948.[68]

The illustrious writer is certainly an important reference if one wants to offer visibility to a text; beyond that, Duhamel, doctor, witness and amateur musician, represented an excellent choice. Duhamel, who wrote *Vie des Martyrs* in 1917 (immediately translated as *The new book of martyrs*, Toronto: J.M. Dent, 1918) and *Civilisation, 1914-1917* in 1918, which won the Prix Goncourt that year (*Civilization, 1914-1917*, New York: The Century Co., 1919), was one of the inventors of the literature of the Great War, a war that was barely 25 years old. Laks also perceived the importance of the Great War, "sacred" to the Nazis; he recounts the episode of the song "Argonner Wald", loved by one SS music lover for its victorious campaign in the Argonne in 1915, but banned by another because of the 1918 defeat. He comes back to this even more clearly in an interview dating from 1972: "*One day we foolishly started a march called 'Argonne Forest' and right in the middle an orderly asked us to stop and change the march: it was sacred music, if you like.*"[69]

Duhamel had already spoken out in the 1930s to describe the Nazis' "doomed enterprise" against the Jews: "For the leaders of the Third Reich, it is a matter of isolating the Jews, expropriating them, starving them, forcing them into despair and suicide. (...) It is as a biologist that I take the liberty of announcing this to them. A Germany, even an all-powerful one, which would be mistress of Europe, (...) could not abolish a people of at least twenty million inhabitants, a people scattered throughout all the nations of the earth (...)"[70]

In 1940, in a front-page article in Le *Figaro* entitled "Imagerie biologique" (*Biological Imagery*), Duhamel reiterated that the

Nazis, already victorious in Poland and only a few days away from the offensive in France, were spreading "a very serious disease (...) a fearsome infection. (...) The infecting agent, as the biologists say, has its starting point in the German people. (...) We must be prepared for the infection to spread to other organs, one by one." Faced with these "serious complications", these "metastases", whose prescience could only be largely euphemistic, Dr. Duhamel dared to formulate some prescriptions, because "the foreseeable end is the failure of the forces of resistance, and that is death. Needless to say, I'm not even talking about France here. What risks dying is an entire world, with its works, its doctrines, its morals, its religions, all its spiritual and temporal treasures. It also goes without saying that, in such cases, the infectious agent usually succumbs with the organism it has killed. But this atrocious justice is no consolation to philosophers. So, no hesitation, it remains for us to do everything we can to bring about a complete cure."[71]

In 1948, Duhamel opened his preface with the same biological metaphor: "madmen and sick people to whom for twenty years the Germanic world has handed over its destinies, (...) a crisis of cruel dementia which has perverted almost an entire people." But even though he insisted on "Mephistopheles (...), the figure, constantly revived, of a truly national hero,"[72] he was totally shaken. All his life, he had been searching for universal human values and looking for medical, psychiatric reasons for the deviations of some people. Reading *Musiques d'un autre monde* revealed to him that he had been dramatically mistaken. His theories on the madness that had seized the Germans were no longer tenable.

The humanist music lover takes up the pen. If he no longer has any "element of consolation" to look forward to, it's not because he's read the descriptions of extermination in the gas chambers, which don't hold his interest—which symptomatic for the period:

one knows, but does not dwell on. No, what revolted him was exactly what the composer Simon Laks, whom he had read, said: the discovery of *"music in a Nazi concentration camp"*—we should also say "extermination center", Auschwitz and Birkenau—and what it meant.

During both world wars, music played an important role for Duhamel. He played between operations during the first war, and in 1944 published an essay, *La musique consolatrice* (*Consolatory Music*),[73] in which he focused on two German composers, Bach and Wagner. The title of Laks and Coudy's manuscript was certainly a major factor in his willingness to read it, as he was bound to be inundated with requests. But what he found there was not that "our last refuges were spared in this universal disaster," but on the contrary, that "holy music, divine music (was) also compromised in the adventure."[74]

All that remained was despair; Duhamel, the doctor, would never find a cure for this ailment "of their desperate genius."

## "MUCH HAS BEEN WRITTEN ABOUT THE NAZI CAMPS, AND WE DO NOT THINK IT IS NECESSARY TO ADD ANY NEW, EVEN UNPUBLISHED, DOCUMENTS."[75]

As Laks and Coudy a flood of information has poured in since 1945 about Nazi atrocities. So why bear witness again? Because *"despite the quantity of books that have been published, despite even the films made about the concentration camps, my interlocutors are always amazed every time I talk to them about Auschwitz in general and its musical activity in particular."*[76]

*Auschwitz* in general: Duhamel himself does not distinguish in his preface between concentration camp and extermination center, Auschwitz and Birkenau. Only the camp's miraculous survivors could write about both the chance events that made them survivors, and the certainty of the experience's incommunicability: "*Everything happened there in a universe of infinity. (...) Beyond a certain limit, human suffering ceases to be perceptible and definable for those who have not gone beyond it. We who 'saw it' did not want to believe, neither at the beginning nor later, that it was possible. How, then, could the authenticity of the facts be accepted by those who had not witnessed them?*"[77] Was it because of the saturation—150 accounts of Auschwitz were published in France alone between 1945 and 1949—the impossibility of perceiving what was being said, the return to normal life at a time when the most pervasive consequences of the war seemed to be fading away? The book was lucky enough to find a major publisher and a famous preface, and yet it did not sell, despite rare reviews, admittedly limited to the Resistance and even Communist press at the time of the definitive formation of the two blocs: "There can be no peace without the demilitarization and denazification of Hitler's guilty and defeated Germany. To all those who forget without remorse this past of shame for humanity, it is appropriate to recall Auschwitz, and the musicians commissioned to accompany the torment of the victims in the crematoria."[78] In this Polish newspaper, there is no Birkenau, no gas chambers, and no concern to respect the authors' statement that they played for the comings and goings of the work commandos.

Simon Laks also returns to "normal" life. He got married, had a child—André, his name in *Music From Another World*—started composing again, first very intermittently, then intensively, in the early 1960s. And it's in this capacity that we find him in the newspaper columns. In 1963, music critic Jacques Lonchampt crushed the over-aged winner of the Divonne-les-Bains composition competition with his contempt in *Le Monde*: "A dismaying evening at Salle Gaveau (...) The composers' jury awarded the grand prize of 5,000 francs to Simon Laks (aged sixty), in which there is a little fantasy, a lot of banality and an English horn solo that would make Wagner swoon."[79] The composer's past is ignored, the reference to Wagner—a favorite of the Nazis—is devoid of irony...

And yet, for over a decade now, the composer Simon Laks has won against the "avant-garde" critic, as the musicologist Frank Harders-Wuthenow, who has edited and resurrected his work, like that of many other excellent musicians swallowed up by the 20th century, shows in the present volume. It's as if it had taken the same amount of time to discover the reality of the Shoah and the singular talent of a composer who could easily have been one among so many of its victims.

What did Simon Laks think? The French Republic recognized him—in 1957!—as a "political deportee". Laks continued to seek precise information from the International Red Cross Research Service in Arolsen well into the 1960s. His correspondence, his readings—everything proves that he never stopped reflecting on his experience in Birkenau, even if he did not frequent the organizations of former deportees in France.

In 1972, an exchange with *Mercure de France*—now part of Gallimard—informed him after three years of procrastination (his first letter requesting copies dated from 1967) that the book had been scrapped. Simon Laks is "outraged and scandalized. That you did not see fit, either commercially or as a matter of pure intellectual courtesy, to warn me of this destruction, nor to offer to buy back a certain number of copies, is beyond my comprehension."[80] Simon Laks appealed to UNESCO for expert advice, and the organization bluntly reminded the publisher of his duties towards his authors. Le *Mercure* sends a pitiful letter to Simon Laks, with a check for a contemptible amount, "the book's mediocre situation and its very low circulation—and this curt politeness, "I hope that your book, if republished, will finally meet with satisfactory success."[81] In December 1972, Le Mercure/Gallimard showed no interest whatsoever in such a remarkable book on Auschwitz-Birkenau. In 1972, the year in which Barbie's extradition was requested from Bolivia following Beate and Serge Klarsfeld's militant hunt, the year in which the revelation of Touvier's pardon provoked an outcry in France, in the early seventies when people began to think seriously about the Jewish specificity of Auschwitz, such as a young intellectual, Pierre Vidal-Naquet, who would write a preface to *Mélodies d'Auschwitz* twenty years later.[82] This is the book, an updated version of the 1948 *Musiques d'un autre monde* that Simon Laks, after having tried in vain to get hold of René Coudy,[83] decided to publish in Polish under his own name and under a different title.

## *"AND NOTHING WILL STOP THEM". BETWEEN "ZONE GRISE" AND THE ASSASSINS ARE AMONG US.*

In the 1970s, Simon Laks reflected with former camp musicians on their shared experience, and read a great deal of publications that inspired him or against whom he wanted to react. Having died in 1983, he could not have been aware of the polemics about the grey zone that overshadowed Primo Levi's last years and continued after his death; indeed, the whole issue only came to light very late. But Laks' correspondence with Simon Wiesenthal and Hermann Langbein[84] shows how closely he followed all the international debates on survivors' testimony. What's more, as early as *Musiques d'un autre monde* (1948), perfectly synchronized with *If this is a man* and the chapter entitled *Shipwrecked and Survivors* (which was Levi's first choice for the book because of its Dantesque origin),[85] Simon Laks and René Coudy had perfectly expressed in the same way the ambiguities that made survival possible and thus induce the "guilt"[86] of survivors. They adapted these contradictions to their very specific condition as musicians, artists in the service of the executioners:

art, at once misappropriated and not, had signified their survival. If factory prisoners—and particularly those in the IG Farben complex, divided into numerous commandos, with the immense Monowitz at its center—could resist by sabotaging their workpieces to slow down the Nazi war effort, the forced musicians tried to play well or even just right: their human resistance came through their creation; but this creation appealed to the SS, who—at least for some of them—differentiated between good and bad music. "*Are men who love music so much, men who cry when they listen to it, capable of doing so much harm, of doing harm at all? Alas! The charm dissipates as soon as the music stops. And the man reverts to what he really is: a* Kraut*, a monster.*"[87] The perversion of certain SS men is pushed to the limit when their desire for music alternates savage assassinatios: one loves Jewish music, another, Gypsy music, the last one, jazz, the music of black Americans, one of the most "degenerate", to be sure.[88]

This very subtle analysis and extreme lucidity of the relationship of internees with executioners and survival is what makes Simon Laks so original in the immense literature of the concentration camps. To eat, to quench one's thirst, not to work outside, is to live: for the camp is nothing but death, still death, barring a "*miracle*." This is what Laks said again in 1975 to Hermann Langbein, whose *Men and Women at Auschwitz* he had just enjoyed:[89] "An immense work of documentation and study, an impartiality so difficult to adopt in this field. My heartiest congratulations! (...) The only reservation I have relates to the chapter on 'Resistance'. (...) You describe as acts of 'resistance' such acts as: escapes, helping starving comrades, religious convictions, hiding someone before a selection, providing information outside the camp, etc. For me, all these actions aim at 'saving one's skin'—or that of a loved one—and are not 'resistance' in the sense it's generally understood. Sabotage—yes, that's resistance: but was it organized and systematic? Not as far as I know. It was just sporadic, individual action. (...) To risk one's life by engaging in such acts? We risked it any way we could, all the time, 24 hours a day."[90]

Simon Laks, an eyewitness to absolute evil, set the highest ethical standards: he saw the horror, experienced the suffering inflicted, and decided to do everything in his power to bear witness to it. He became paradigmatic of the figure of the "moral witness" invented by Avishai Margolit.[91] From Nuremberg onwards, or at least when he thought back to it in the 1980s, Laks understood, like the young Raphaël Lemkin at the time of the trial of the Armenian Tehlirian for the assassination of Tallaat Pasha in 1921, that those responsible for genocide cannot really be judged. "For the penal code states—in all civilized countries—that 'punishment must be proportional to the crime committed', and consequently the said code has established that the premeditated murder of *a* person is punishable by the supreme penalty, i.e. death or life imprisonment. Hitler's crimes should have given a new face to the administration of justice: 'If the murder of one person is punishable *by the highest* penalty, then how can the murder of hundreds, thousands, millions of human beings be punished? Faced with such an accusation, the judgments handed down at Nuremberg in 1945-46 have the character of a tragic farce, or at best a hollow symbol."[92] This is why Laks attacks Simon Wiesenthal, against the 'hollow symbol' of the trials he multiplies and his literature. Even though he did not want to militate with Hermann Langbein, who tirelessly convened the international organization of camp elders from Vienna, he corresponded with him and shared his "moral reservations" about Wiesenthal. Of course, Laks admires the famous Nazi hunter: "Wiesenthal's merits are innumerable, and they arouse all the more admiration because he has given up his lucrative and safe profession as an architect to undertake the thankless and risky mission of righting wrongs that are so difficult, and indeed impossible, to right. And what follows is: impossible to punish."[93]

But Laks remains highly skeptical of Wiesenthal as a *pro domo* writer; he criticizes *Max and Helen* at length, in which the ruthless hunter tells of having given up pursuing a murderer in this one case to protect Helen, raped by this SS man, because she had had a son by him, totally unaware of his origin. Laks questions Wiesenthal's moral stance: why make an exception out of millions of cases? In another fictional account, *The Sunflower,* Wiesenthal asks whether a Jew should grant forgiveness to a dying Christian SS man who asks for it.[94] The book is all the more twisted because, playing on his notoriety, Wiesenthal asks a number of personalities—philosophers, writers, Christians, Jews—to answer the question. We have those of Primo Levi and Vercors. Both raise the question of the naivety and perversity of the SS, and that of the author. This is probably what Simon Laks would also have concluded. For he distances himself above all from Wiesenthal in his conviction that trials can prevent neither Holocaust denial nor reiteration. Even so, he died in 1983, after 1975 and the Cambodia of the Khmer Rouge, but before 1994 and the genocide of the Tutsis in Rwanda and that of the Bosnians in Srebrenica. "A pointless effort. There will always be Faurissons. Second pointless effort. Numerous trials have already taken place, starting with the Nuremberg trials. None has stopped the assassins to come. And nothing will stop them."[95]

*"But how do you explain that one part of humanity could resolve to coldly destroy another? It seems to me so monstrous, so incompatible with... the universal conception of morality...*

*—It's obvious, but someone had to think of it.*

*And the German thought of it. You just have to understand the principle. Have you ever felt remorse at crushing a louse? To the Germans we are lice."*[96]

# NOTES

1. *AM*, p. 7. For the partial shift of perspective between the two versions, see André Laks' contribution, above, p. 144.

2. See Pascal Quignard, *The Hatred of Music*, New Haven : Yale University Press, 2016, who refers p. 129 to a specific episode that features in *AM*, p. 98-99, and above, p. 164 and note 38. For recent works concerning the relationship between art and survival in Nazis concentration and extermination camps, especially poetry, see, among others, Rachel Ertel, *Dans la langue de personne, poésie yiddish de l'anéantissement*, Paris: Seuil, 1993, and the magnificent catalog of the exhibition of the same name, at the Musée de Belfort in 2015: *Retour sur l'abîme : l'art à l'épreuve du génocide,* Mare & Martin, 2015 (with texts by Jean-Christophe Bailly, Hélène Cixous, Philippe Cyroulnik, Nicolas Surlapierre, Pierre Wat); *Art, Music and Education as Strategies for Survival, Theresienstadt* 1941-45 (Anne D. Dutlinger, ed.), New-York: Herodias, 2000.

3. The documentation is preserved in Simon Laks' Archive (Polish Library in Paris) and in André Laks' personal Archive.

4. I use Coudy for the author, Khoudy for the man (see below, n. 6).

5. Jean Samuel (with Jean-Marc Dreyfus), *Il m'appelait Pikolo, un compagnon de Primo Levi raconte,* Paris : Robert Laffont, 2007. Note that Primo Levi's first book, published in Italy in 1947*, Rapporto sull'organizzazione igienico-sanitaria del campo di concentramento per ebrei di Monowitz (Auschwitz, Alta Silesia* , was written by Primo-Levi, chemist, with a fellow doctor, Leonardo Debenetti, physician-surgeon (*Auschwitz report*, trans. Judith Woolf, New York : Verso, 2006).

6. Precise documentation on Simon (Szymon) Laks and his 1948 co-author René Coudy (spelled Khoudy) was found in the archives of the *International Tracing Service* in Bad Alrosen, which compiles all camp data and family tracing by Jan Lambertz of the *United States Holocaust Memorial Museum*. My warmest thanks to her. See the Red Cross documents reproduced here, p. 162.)

7. Eichmann reported to Reinhard Heydrich head of the *Reich Central Security Office (RSHA)*.

8. File compiled by André Tulard, civil administrator and deputy, director of the "Service des étrangers" of the Paris police headquarters, which under Vichy became the "Service des étrangers et des affaires juives." The file is now housed in an enclave of the National Archives at the Shoah Memorial in Paris.

9. Charles Minczeles to "My dear little wife and children" and Jukiel Obarzanek to his "dear family" on July 16, 1942, in Antoine Mercier, *Convoi n° 6. Destination Auschwitz July 17, 1942*, Le Cherche Midi, 2005, p.86 and p.42. For "degenerate art" and the organization of these deportations, see Annette Becker, *Des Juifs trahis par leur France, 1939-1944,* Gallimard, 2024.

10. In "Auschwitz and the Polish Jews", chapter 11 of *Les Polonais et la Shoah, a new historiographical school* (A. Kichelewski, J.Lyon-Caen, J C. Szurek, A.Wieviorka (dir.), CNRS éditions, 2019, Tal Bruttmann shows that Polish Jews were the first contingent of Jews deported to Auschwitz and then Birkenau, and the most numerous murdered there after Jews from Hungary. This included Poles from abroad, such as Simon Laks, who had since long settled in Paris as a musician. For those selected to work in the camp, knowledge of Polish—as well as German and Yiddish—was obviously an asset.

11. *AM,* p. 20.

12. Above, p. 15.

13. *AM,* p. 23.

14. *The Pilecki Report. Voluntary deportee to Auschwitz, 1940-1943*, Époques Champ Vallon, 2014. (Drafted summer 1945). Witold Pilecki, *The Auschwitz Volunteer: Beyond Bravery,* Aquila Polonica, 2012.

15. *AM,* p. 21.

16. I borrow the expression from Jorge Semprun.

17. Letter to Himmler, September 18, 1942, quoted in Sybille Steinbacher, *Auschwitz, A History,* Penguin books, 2004. (German original, 2005).

18. Above, p. 26.

19. Jacques Sémelin, *Purifier et détruire, Usages politiques des massacres et génocides,* Seuil, 2005. *Purify and Destroy: The Political Uses of Massacre and Genocide*, Columbia University Press, 2009.

20. Above, p. 23f.

21. Above, p. 113. The virtuoso violinist of the orchestra, Gustav Mahler's niece Alma, had been moved to Block 10, the block of medical experimentation, because the camp commandant Mandel insisted on good music. See also Élise Petit, *Musique et politique en Allemagne, du IIIe Reich à l'aube de la Guerre froide*, Presses Universitaires / Paris Sorbonne, 2018.

22. Piotr Rawicz, Polish Jew and Auschwitz survivor, author of the novel *Blood from the Sky,* Yale University Press, paperback, 2003 (*Le Sang du ciel*, Gallimard, 1961), testifies in Michel Huillard's film "Le Survivant de Varsovie" (The Warsaw Srurvivor), broadcasted on May 5, 1972 on the French first television channel (Archives INA, BNF).

23. *AM,* p. 17.

24. Primo Levi, *Survival in Auschwitz : if this is a man* (trans. Stuart Woolf ), New York, Orion Press, 2008, p. 25.

25. Primo Levi, *ibid.*, p. 52.

26. Juliane Brauer, "How Can Music Be Torturous? Music in Nazi Concentration and Extermination Camps", *Music & Politics*, vol. X/1, 2016.

27. *AM,* p.17.

28. *AM,* p. 31f. and p.34.

29. *AM*, p. 34.

30. Above, p. 94. On the spoliation of music instruments during the Shoah, see Annette Becker, "Spolier les âmes : les musiciens et leurs instruments devant les chambres à gaz", in the dossier "La spoliation des instruments de musique dans la Shoah : premières recherches", *Revue d'Histoire de la Shoah*, n°213, March 2021, p.143-158.

31. *AM* p. 94.

32. *AM*, p. 32f.

33. Mieczysław Kościelniak, the Polish painter interned at Auschwitz as early as 1941, often depicted musicians and their instruments in his clandestine work, which was saved by the camp resistance and then in the 1950s. Thus the women's orchestra, with cello and violins playing in front of female prisoners leaving for forced labor, their leader baton in hand. In the distance, the immense smoke of a crematorium. http://denktag2006.denktagarchiv.de/typo3temp/pics/4f904e3a1e.jpg .

34. Bruno Giner, *Survivre et mourir en musique dans les camps nazis* (*Surviving and Dying to Music in the Nazi Camps*), Berg International, 2011, p. 154.

35. Some witnesses, especially from other camps, speak of executions to music. But Primo Levi confirms Simon Laks. After the revolt of the Birkenau *Sonderkommando*, the marching band withdrew after the usual musical entrance of the prisoners to the roll-call square, where a hanging took place; he insists on silence (*Op. cit.* above, n. 24, p. 177)

36. *AM*, p.58.

37. Interview in "The Warsaw Survivor" (see above, n. 22).

38. Pelagia Lewinska, *Twenty Months in Auschwitz*, Nagel, 1966, p.94. (New-York, 1968).

39. Above, p. 105.

40. Above, p. 78.

41. Above, p. 39f.

42. Above, p. 64.

43. Above, p. 81.

44. Above, p. 85.

45. Above, p. 87.

46. Above, p. 66.

47. Above, p. 32.

48. Above, p. 120.

49. Above, p. 87.

50. Above, p. 97f.

51. *Ibid.*

52. Above, p. 67f.

53. The ICRC did not make much effort to understand, as the report by delegate Maurice Rossel in 1944 shows. See Christine Rütten's documentary, *La Croix-Rouge sous le IIIe Reich, histoire d'un échec* (2006), and Isabelle Vonèche-Cardia, *Neutralité et engagement, les relations entre le Comité international de la Croix-Rouge (CICR) et le Gouvernement suisse, 1938-1945,* Lausanne, Société d'histoire de la Suisse romande, 2012. Sébastien Farré and Yan Schubert, in "L'illusion de l'objectif. Le délégué du CICR Maurice Rossel et les photographies de Theresienstadt", *Le Mouvement social,* 2009/2 n°227, p.65 to 83, have brought a lot of new light to bear on the photographs taken by Rossel under the supervision of the SS. Not surprisingly, there are images of musicians and instruments, including a rehearsal of Verdi's *Requiem* and a bandstand. The first Polish fiction films made after the genocide often feature instruments, too; for example, *The Last Stage* by Wanda Jakubowska (1948), herself an Auschwitz survivor, or *The Passenger* (1963) by Andrzej Munk and Witold Lesiewicz.

54. Above, p. 68.

55. Above, p. 109.

56. Above, p. 103.

57. *AM*, p. 130.

58. Daniel Blatman, *The Death Marches. The Final Phase of Nazi Genocide,* Harvard University Press, 2013 (*Les Marches de la mort, la dernière étape du génocide nazi, Paris,* Fayard, 2009).

59. Above, p. 75.

60. Above, p. 171.

61. Aharon Appelfeld, *The story of a life*, translated from the Hebrew by Aloma Halter, New York : Schocken Books, 2004. The refugees in question are survivors of the Kaltchund concentration camp in the Ukraine, who speak of the 'Keffer' enclosure where the SS fed hungry wolfhounds with children.

62. This is the last strophe of the poem "Aschenglorie", in *Atemwende* (1967); see Pierre Joris' translation in Paul Celan, *Breathturn*, Los Angeles : Sun & Moon Press, 1995.

63. Above, p. 123.

64. *AM*, p. 124. Compare Imre Kertesz, the future Nobel Prize winner, in *Fatelessness* (New York : Vintage International, 2004): "And despite reflection, reason, discernment, common sense, I could not ignore the voice of a kind of deaf desire, which had crept into me, as if ashamed to be so senseless, and yet more and more obstinate: I wanted to live a little longer in this beautiful concentration camp."

65. "An exceptional supplementary prize of 50,000 francs was awarded to Simon Laks and René Coudy for their story *Musiques d'un autre monde* (...) They recounted their odyssey in the Auschwitz deportation camp, where they were assigned to the musicians' *kommando*". *Le Monde,* 13/11/1947.

66. Ironically, the magazine *Le Mercure de France* was banned because its director, Jacques-Alexandre Bernard, who had replaced Duhamel, was sentenced in July 1945 to 5 years' imprisonment for "intelligence with the enemy". Throughout the Occupation, he had maintained "intimate relations with the propaganda services": "Of pro-Hitler sentiment, Bernard placed himself, after the armistice, at the disposal of the Germans in order to publish, in place of the magazine which had ceased publication since June 1, 1940, the propaganda works they wished to see published in France. (...) It was to publish Dr. Rosenberg's *Myth of the Twentieth Century*, the bible of Nazism, and if the work did not leave the Mercure de France presses, this was due to the patriotism of the typographers who delayed the work. Jacques-Alexandre Bernard, (...) in response to President Ledoux's questions, simply cited the anti-German or anti-fascist works he had published before the war, but he had to admit that he was 'inclined' towards Hitler, because, he said, he was a 'friend of order'" (*Le Monde,* 17-07-1947). Bernard had tried to buy the shares owned by Georges Duhamel, in order to become the main shareholder, before having the writer's works pillaged. In 1945, Duhamel entrusted the *Revue* to the resistance fighter Paul Hartman, and the publishing house resumed (see Duhamel, *Livre de l'amertume*, Mercure de France, 1983).

67. Surprisingly, François Azouvi does not mention Duhamel in his book *Le Mythe du grand silence, Auschwitz, les Français, la mémoire,* Paris: Fayard, 2012.

68. Correspondence between Laks and Duhamel's secretariat, November 18, 1947 to January 15, 1948, in which Laks expresses his "Profound gratitude" to "Monsieur et cher Maître" for the preface "from his illustrious pen."

69. *AM,* p. 71; Film "The Warsaw Survivor" (cf. above, n. 28).

70. *Le Figaro,* June 23, 1938. I warmly thank Pauline Breton, author of the thesis (Paris-Nanterre, 2015, dir. Annette Becker and Laurence Campa) for her indications and suggestions.

71. *Le Figaro,* May 7 1940, front page and p. 3.

72. Above, p. 11.

73. G. Duhamel, *La Musique consolatrice*, Éditions du Rocher, 1944.

74. Above, p. 12.

75. Above, p. 14. It is this passage that Annette Wieviorka quotes in her book *Déportation et génocide, entre la mémoire et l'oubli,* Plon, 1992, in which she demonstrates that deportees testified a great deal at first, then did so less and less in the 1950s, because they thought they were inaudible; recent work partly invalidates this observation. Cf. Azouvi, *op.cit.* (above, n. 67) Philip Nord, *After the Deportation, Memory Battles in Postwar France,* Cambridge University Press, 2020.

76. Above, p. 14.

77. Above, p. 14f.

78. *Friends of Poland, August/September* 1948.

79. *Le Monde,* 02/11/1963. A year later, at the audition in Divonne, there was no respite: "This Concerto is a short work, which unfolds in its three traditional parts its amiable lines, of easy invention though sometimes short of breath. Memories of the Ravelian style float here and there. Nothing aggressive; nothing new either. A single desire: to please; which explains the great success, shared by the performer, Annie d'Arco, international piano prizewinner, Geneva 1946." (14/07/1964). The *Concerto* in question is the *Concerto da camera* for piano, 9 wind instruments and percussion (see André Laks's contribution, above).

80. Letter from S. Laks to the literary director of Mercure de France, September 16, 1972.

81. Letter from *Mercure de* France to Simon Laks, December 5, 1972.

82. F. Azouvi, *op. cit.* (above, n. 67), p. 250-270. For P. Vidal-Naquet's Preface, see above, Editorial Notice, p. 8, n. 2.

83. From 1973 onwards, Simon Laks was looking for René Coudy for "possible reprints", and even put a wanted notice in the newspaper *Le Déporté* in 1974. To no avail.

84. André Laks' Archives.

85. Dante has become a topos of reflection on Auschwitz, as Simon Laks put it in 1972: "We were entering a Dantesque world, weren't we, and it took several months to fully understand where we had landed", interview in the film "The Warsaw Survivor", op.cit.

86. Not to be confused with "survivor syndrome", an acute condition suffered by a number of camp survivors and invented by New York psychiatrist William Niederland in 1961. See Bruno Cabanes, "Le complexe du survivant, histoire et usages d'une notion" in Bruno Cabanes and Guillaume Picketty (eds), *Retours à l'intime au sortant de la guerre,* Seuil, 2010; William Niederland "The Survivor Syndrome: Further Observations and Dimensions", *Journal of the Psychoanalytic Association,* vol.29/2, April 1981.

87. Above, p. 115.

88. Simon Laks devotes a paragraph to Pery Broad, of the camp's Gestapo, responsible in particular for recruiting " *a certain number of female prisoners for a brothel the authorities had established in Auschwitz 1*) and for "*a trifle: the burning of a few thousand Gypsies and then the same number of Czechs.*" (*AM*, p. 82), accordionist of genius, tried in Frankfurt in 1964-1965: " *As far as I know, no one has mentioned his uncommon musical talents, not as a way of bringing him mitigating circumstances, but simply as an example of a rarely seen combination—is it typically Teutonic? - of unbridled criminality and the heights of artistry.*" *AM*, p. 80 (cf. also above, p. 119-21).

89. H. Langbein, *People in Auschwitz,* University of North Carolina Press, 2004 (originally in German , *Menschen in Auschwitz* 1972. Langbein, he claims, used the word "human beings" so as not to demonize even the SS. As early as 1947-48, he had written an account which, despite his difficulties in publishing it, appeared under the title *Die Stärkeren: Ein Bericht* in 1949) Hermann Langbein devotes a few paragraphs to the Birkenau concerts in Chapter II, 4, "Music and Games", and cites Laks and Coudy's book , p. 136.

90. Letter from S. Laks to H. Langbein, June 2, 1975 (André Laks' Archives). In the same letter, Simon Laks refers to Józef Garlinski's 1974 Polish book, *Oświęcim walczący* (in English: *Fighting Auschwitz : the resistance movement in the concentration camp*, Fawcett Publications, 1975), whose chapter on resistance he also disputes.

91. A. Margolit, *The Ethics of Memory*, Harvard University Press, 2004.

92. Simon Laks on S. Wiesenthal's *Max and Helen*, in *Mélodies d'Auschwitz et autres écrits sur les camps*, Cerf 2018, Appendix 3, p. 353. The passage is an extract from S. Laks, *Moja wojna o pokój* (*My War for Peace*), *Oficyna Poetów i Malarzy*, London, 1983, p. 77-87 (trans. André Laks).

93. Simon Laks, *ibid.*, p. 352s.

94. Simon Wiesenthal, *The Sunflower*, London : W.H. Allen 1970.

95. Simon Laks, *ibid.* (above, n. 92), p. 353. Laks knew, like Raphaël Lemkin, that one never emerges unscathed from genocide: "After a war, even a lost one, a nation can rebuild its technical and financial resources, start a new life. But those destroyed in genocide are lost forever. The losses of war can be repaired; the losses of genocide are irreparable." Lemkin Archives, *New York Public Library*. Microfilm 2, 1950. Annette Becker, *Messengers of Disaster, Raphaël Lemkin, Jan Karski and Twentieth-Century Genocides,* The University of Wisconsin Press, 2021.

96. Above, p. 82.

Frank Harders-Wuthenow
# THE COMPOSER SIMON LAKS
(1901-1983)[1]

Szymon Laks was born on November 1, 1901 in Warsaw, the city on the Vistula under the rule of the Tsarist Empire, into an assimilated Jewish family. His father Isaac sold insurance. His mother, Sarah Chelemer, the daughter of a wine merchant, supported the family by giving Polish lessons. In addition to his elder brother Henryk, the family also included younger siblings Leo, Anne, and David. Although the grandfather on his father's side was a rabbi, religion played little role in the family home. The transmission of Jewish culture was ensured by music, which was omnipresent. Jewish folk songs were among Szymon's earliest musical memories, associated with his mother's wonderful voice. He would pay tribute to them with *Eight Jewish Folk Songs* in 1947. Sarah Laks took care of her children's musical training. Szymon began learning the violin at the age of four, and soon took up the piano. He seemed predestined for a career as a musician; after graduating from high school, however, he enrolled at Vilnius University in mathematics, before studying composition and conducting at the Warsaw Academy of Music between 1921 and 1924. It must not have been easy for him to secure a place, as there was a *numerus clausus* (limited places) for Jews, who were treated as foreigners. Only the best were accepted, and they had to be better than their "Polish" classmates. They had to take extra exams and face tougher tests. Szymon left Poland after completing his studies, but

---

1. Postface to the re-edition of the German translation of *Gry oświęcimskie*, *Musik in Auschwitz* (Berlin 2024/2028), revised for the present publication.

this was not due solely to the anti-Semitic climate.² Opportunities for artistic development and professional prospects were simply lacking.

Laks left a country not to be found on the political map of Europe. It was "in Poland, that is to say, nowhere," that Alfred Jarry set the action of his provocative play *King Ubu*.³ Indeed, when the play premiered in 1896, Poland's identity was in crisis and on the edge of oblivion. For generations, any desire for independence had been nipped in the bud. Resistance fighters and troublesome opponents ended up in the gulags, the labor camps of Siberia.⁴ A large part of the political and intellectual elite lived in exile. Many sought to put pressure (with the help of lobbies) on the world's powerful to try and win them over to Poland's cause. At their head was one of the stars of the time, pianist and composer Ignacy Paderewski. Due to Paderewski's extraordinary diplomatic skills, U.S. President Woodrow Wilson, at the end of the First World War, included the reconstruction of the Polish state in his 14-point plan for a new European order.

For the three million Polish Jews, who in 1918 made up around a tenth of the country's population, the return to sovereignty of the Polish state, whose first president was Paderewski, was of no immediate

---

2. On the notorious anti-Semitism of Piotr Rytel, for example, one of the teachers at the Academy of Music, with whom Laks also studied, see the memoirs of Andrzej Panufnik (*Composing myself*, London 1987), and Alexandre Tansman (*Regards en arrière*, Château-Gontier, 2013).

3. "As for the action that is about to begin, it takes place in Poland, that is to say, nowhere", wrote Jarry in a lecture given on the occasion of the premiere in December 1896. Further on, he wrote: "Nulle part is everywhere, and the country in which we find ourselves, first of all. That's why Ubu speaks French."

4. For example, Eugeniusz Morawski (1876-1948), unjustly forgotten but one of the most important Polish composers of his generation alongside Szymanowski, took part in the armed resistance against the Tsarist empire and was condemned to exile in Siberia. Fortunately, Morawski was able to exchange the gulag for exile in Paris, because his father bought him out from the Russian administration. He returned to Poland in the 1920s. As director of the Warsaw Academy of Music, he taught a large number of Polish composers destined to become famous, including Grazyna Bacewicz, Witold Lutosławski and Andrzej Panufnik. A great part of his work was lost in the destruction of Warsaw in 1944.

benefit. With the new independence, the old anti-Semitism found its way into the platforms of the conservative parties. It became a dominant tone on the keyboard of nationalism and chauvinism, from which other minorities in Poland also suffered.

In *King Ubu,* a key work of the Theater of the Absurd, Jarry used Poland as the cipher for a fictitious kingdom outside civilization, a place where all values are inverted, where the banality of evil manifests itself in the distorting mirror of the grotesque. In 1942, Simon Laks, later deported from Paris, experienced the actual banality of evil in Auschwitz-Birkenau, a German concentration and extermination camp on Polish soil, a real place outside civilization. He himself described it in the second version of his account of Auschwitz (1979)[5] as "a kind of 'negative' of the world": "white had become black, black white, values had rotated one hundred and eighty degrees."

After a stay in Vienna in the early 1920s, of which there is no record, Szymon followed his brothers Leo and Henryk to Paris in 1926, where he changed his first name to Simon. He passed the entrance exam to the *Conservatoire* and completed his training with Henri Rabaud, director of the Institute, and Pierre Vidal, a pupil of the legendary 'pape de la fugue,'[6] André Gédalge.[7] Laks perfected his skills with an apprenticeship that was to make him a master of contrapuntal forms and instrumental refinement. The final movement of his *Sinfonietta for strings*, composed in Paris in 1936, in which Laks brilliantly and not without irony explores the most complicated

---

5. See above, Editorial Note.
6. Literally, "pope of the fugue."
7. Gédalge, one of the most influential personalities in the French musical world at the beginning of the 20th century, was also of Polish Jewish decent.

fugue techniques, sounds like a retrospective wink to the days of the *Conservatoire*.

Laks earned his living as a café violinist and silent-film accompanist, and published entertaining music under pseudonyms. Like his brother Léo, he signed on as a musician on cruise ships, touring the world in the 20s. In Paris, he had the chance to experience a historic moment for music. The spirit of the times was forging influential trends, and musical elites were setting the tone by forming groups such as the *Groupe des Six* and the *École de Paris*.[8] In the foreground of this favorable backdrop, an ever-growing musical colony was created under the aegis of Piotr Perkowski, a pupil of Symanowski, to form the *Association des Jeunes Musiciens Polonais*, which was to enrich Parisian musical life with original nuances.[9] Laks recalled in 1964, in an interview with musicologist-journalist Tadeusz Kaczyński: "The Society was founded shortly after my arrival in Paris, in 1926. At that time, Perkowski, Sikorski, Rutkowski, Feliks Roderyk Labuński were already members, followed by Sztompka, Kondracki and Gradstein. This nucleus was constantly growing—hence the idea of creating an organization. Thanks to Perkowski's inexhaustible energy and Paderewski's generosity, the organization soon became a reality. Our headquarters was no small thing, but rather a fairly spacious room in the newly-built Salle Pleyel. Here we could not only meet and work, but also organize concerts practically every week, featuring resident and visiting musicians and previewing works composed by members of the Society. These concerts, which we called 'auditions', were a great success with the French public. They continued regularly for many

---

8. See the booklets for the CDs devoted to the music of Simon Laks and other Polish composers of Jewish origin persecuted between 1939 and 1945, on the eda records website www.eda-records.com
9. See Renata Suchowiejko's study on the Association of Young Polish Musicians, published in French translation in 2023 by UT Orpheus: *Paris, capitale musicale polonaise dans l'entre-deux-guerres*.

years, right up to the outbreak of war."[10]

Alongside Paderewski, Artur Rubinstein, Alexandre Tansman, Paweł Kochański, Leopold Stokowski and, as the only non-Polish member, Nadia Boulanger formed the Association's honorary committee. From the outset, Laks played an important role in the administration of the Association, which was soon joined by all the leading Polish musicians. As well as organizing concerts, it functioned essentially as a network to help young Polish musicians gain a foothold in Paris, and as a bridge for the transfer of musical culture between Paris and Warsaw. Laks undoubtedly owed the start of his musical career to the influence of the Association, which attracted not only Polish performers, but also many first-rate French musicians. Among the most important activities in the early years of its existence was a competition in 1928, in which only Polish composers could take part, but whose jury was made up exclusively of non-Polish celebrities: Maurice Ravel, Albert Roussel, Florent Schmitt, und Arthur Honegger. Laks received an award for his *Symphonic Blues*, an orchestral piece which, like other works from this period, and all those previously composed in Warsaw, was destroyed during the war.

In the late 1920s, Laks attracted the attention of renowned performers. The *Quatuor Roth*—the French counterpart to Vienna's Kolisch-Quartett—which specialized in the interpretation of contemporary works, included his now defunct *2nd String Quartet* in its repertoire. His friendship with the Polish pianist of Jewish origin, Vlado Perlemuter, who went down in history as a legendary interpreter of Ravel, led to the 1932 *Cello Sonata*, first performed with Perlemuter by Maurice Maréchal, the most famous French cellist of his generation. This sonata shows a young composer at the peak of his mastery, navigating the tension between tradition and

---

10. *Ruch Muzyczny,* Nr.21, September 1964.

contemporaneity, restoration and innovation, which were all typical of the musical sphere in the 1930s. Laks' music is a combination of various influences: Polish and French, with Slavic and Latin traits: pervasiveness, wit, irony, a tendency to virtuosity, but also great meditative depth, especially in the slow movements. Traditional Polish songs and dances are as present as jazz rhythms and harmonies. The similarity to Ravel is already evident in the names of some movements, such as the *Mouvement perpétual,* of the *Trois pièces de concert*, which was composed for Gérard Hekking, then principal cellist of the Concertgebouw Orchestra and a teacher at the Paris Conservatoire, or in the "Blues" of the *Cello Sonata*. In the third movement of the *Cello Sonata*, on the other hand, with its irregular 5-bar groupings and jazz-like harmonies, one could hear the anticipation of Dave Brubeck's rhythmic whims.

The year 1929 cast a shadow over Laks' work with the *Association des Jeunes Musiciens* Polonais. He had received a commission for a film score from the Polish director Joseph Lejtes. The premiere was an event, as it was the first silent Polish film to be shown in France.[11] The Polish ambassador organized a gala presentation for the cream of the crop of Parisian diplomacy. The jealousy of the association's colleagues spilled over onto Laks: Formal offers for the project should have been officially invited, since —so the argument went— it was a Polish film and the music should have been commissioned by a Polish composer. The leitmotif of his youth in Warsaw—being of Jewish origin and therefore "not Polish"—caught up with Laks in Paris.

A close collaboration developed in the 1930s between Laks and the legendary *chansonnière* Tola Korian, for whom Laks wrote a substantial repertoire, which the singer performed throughout Europe

---

11. *Z dnia na dzień* (*Day by day*), based on the novel of the same title by Ferdynand Goetels; the film was shown in Paris under the title *Marusia*, after the main female character Marusia Radziejowska.

even after the war. Laks, who as a representative of the Polish avant-garde had hitherto only written entertainment music to earn money, was profoundly influenced by his encounter with this extraordinary artist. His meeting with Tola Korian inspired many of his songs, which he composed to texts by important Polish and French poets and which he adapted to the singer's exceptional vocal and expressive potential. In the music, the boundaries between serious music and popular music[12] are blurred. A fine example of this blurring is Julian Tuwim's setting of *Dyzio Marzyciel* (*Dédé the Dreamer*). The poem tells of the gastronomic dreams of a young boy lying lazily on the grass, who sees mountains of cakes and raspberry ice cream in the clouds above him. The music unites the spirit of the cabaret song with the serious refinement of a classical *lied* (a characteristic also typical, of course, in the songs of contemporaries like Poulenc or Milhaud). This is another fine example of Laks' 'dialectic of lightness.' The lightness evoked here —and which Jerzy Lefeld, in his later instrumentation of this song, ironically interprets as "celestial" through the introduction of a celesta—is that of a soap bubble. *Dédé the Dreamer* belongs to the many songs by Laks that were played by Polish radio in the 1960s, sometimes in orchestral arrangements, and entered the repertoire of such important Polish singers as Halina Szymulska, who became Laks' Muse incarnated after the war.

During the outbreak of WW2, Simon and his two brothers Léo and Henry were living in Paris. Laks' father, who had left the family in the thirties, died in Warsaw in 1940. His mother Sarah, who had also remained in Warsaw, and his two younger siblings Anna and David, did not survive the Holocaust. Unlike Léo and Henry, who were able to hide with false papers after the occupation, Laks went to the call for registration of foreign Jews. He was subsequently

---

12. Popular music is also referred to as Light music: a less-serious form of Western classical music, which originated in the 18th and 19th centuries and continues today.

arrested by the Vichy authorities on May 14, 1941, and interned at the Beaune-la-Rolande camp near Orléans. Deportation from Pithiviers to Auschwitz followed on July 17, 1942. Laks received the number 49.543. The first work Laks composed after his return from deportation was a tribute to his destroyed homeland, the *3rd String Quartet* "on Polish folk motifs."[13] In its four movements, Laks drew an imaginary musical map of Poland, gathering songs and dances from all regions, from which he drew the thematic material for the quartet.[14] In 1947, he composed the aforementioned arrangement of the *Eight Jewish Folk Songs*. Two years later he composed the *Ballad* for piano "Homage to Chopin," for a national competition organized to mark the 100th anniversary of the composer's death. And in 1954, during an extended stay in a hospital, he wrote the piece called *Poem for violin and orchestra*, which was not performed during his lifetime.

While Laks worked in his brother Léo's production company, he subtitled films for the French cinema and did many translations himself. He became a specialist in the field, and in 1957 published a small book on the technique and aesthetics of subtitling.[15] In 1960 he experienced a new phase of musical creativity, during which he returned to the French public eye. His *4th String Quartet* won a distinction at the *Quatuor de Liège* competition in 1962, then in 1965 was awarded the *Grand Prix de la Reine Elisabeth* in Brussels. In 1963, his *Concerto da Camera* won a first prize at the *Divonne-les-Bains* chamber music competition. He also wrote Lieder cycles, chamber music, a *Symphony for Strings*, and finally, in 1965, his only opera, *L'Hirondelle inattendue*. This one-act *opéra-bouffe* is based

---

13. It is possible that the 3rd String Quartet is a reconstruction of a string quartet Laks composed in 1944, shortly before the evacuation of Auschwitz.
14. On this point, see Antoni Buchner's study of the *3rd Quartet* @www.Boosey.com/Laks.
15. *Le Sous-titrage. Sa technique—son esthétique*, Publication à compte d'auteur, Paris 1957. Reprinted online by J.-F. Cornu in *Écran traduit* (Numéro spécial 1, 2013) @ http://ataa.fr/revue/

on a collection of stories that writer Claude Aveline had written in 1952 as a series for French radio.[16] Aveline, a member of the French Resistance during WW2, was a brilliant and influential figure in the post-war literary scene. His *Bestiaire inattendu* tells the fates of legendary animals such as Jonah's Whale, Prometheus' Eagle and the Manger's Donkey; the perspective adopted is that of the animals themselves, unmasking traditional stories as pure mystifications. The opera begins with the forced landing of a rocket in the Paradise of Famous Animals. A reporter on an interplanetary mission descends. The dove from Noah's Ark welcomes him and his pilot, and introduces them to the inhabitants of the place—all the animals immortalized in myths, legends, stories and literature: the Paradise Serpent, Bern's Bear, Aeschylus' Tortoise, Schubert's Trout, the Hound of the Baskervilles, and so on. Only Jonah's Whale remains invisible—it is too big to be on stage. The presentation is interrupted by the honking of the Capitol Geese, announcing the arrival of a newcomer at the gates of Paradise. The surprise is palpable, and quickly turns to indignation when a ragged creature appears. The animals feel their honor has been wounded. Either the arrival of the newcomer is a mistake, or their days in Paradise are numbered. The young woman always utters the same three sentences: "They call me the swallow of the suburb; I'm just a poor lovechild, born one day in the spring season to a little worker. Like the others, I might have turned out well, if my father, instead of abandoning me, had protected me with his wing." What needs explanation for a non-French audience is obvious to a French

---

16. Claude Aveline, whose real name was Eugen Avtsine, was born in Paris in 1901 to a family of Russian emigrants of Jewish origin. The family acquired French nationality in 1905. The radio version of *Le Bestiaire inattendu* won the Prix Italia in 1955, and was published in book form in 1959 by Mercure de France. Laks also set to music *L'Oiseau qui n'existe pas*, a poem by Aveline dating from 1950 and thematically close to the opera, which has been translated into over fifty languages and, at Aveline's instigation, inspired numerous illustrators and painters. This collection, which Aveline donated to the Musée d'Art Moderne in Paris in the 1970s, is now part of the Centre Pompidou collection.

one. Indeed, "*L'Hirondelle du Faubourg*" is a famous French song from 1912, a "hit" that French audiences could have sung along to when the opera was composed, had it been staged at the time.[17] The song tells the story of a young prostitute who has been stabbed by a client. At the hospital, the attending physician recognizes her from an amulet as the child he had from an affair with a worker he had abandoned. The opera begins when the song ends—with the girl's death and her ascent to heaven. The situation becomes more complicated when Pierre, at the gateway to the humans' Paradise, announces the arrival of a young woman who appears to be identical to the one in the animals' Paradise. At this point, however, the double swallow of the suburb disintegrates in the air, and the reporter gives the solution to the mystery: "This so-called swallow is not a swallow, it's not a woman, it's not a bird, but something much more beautiful: it's a song." To the objection that a song is not something that exists, he replies: "Yes, a song does exist, since it is sung all over the world… Yes, the song is everywhere, whereas we, beasts and men, are only where we are." In the libretto adaptation of Aveline's story, the hidden potential of the story becomes manifest: Only in a different musical context can the song be understood as a musical foreign body. The contempt of the "great animals" for the swallow can thus become a metaphor for contemporary avant-garde music's contempt for song, especially popular song. As the "great animals"—representatives of serious music—welcome the song by singing it themselves, the gap between serious music and lighthearted music is bridged, a gap that

---

17. The opera was first performed in 1975 in a Polish Television production studio. The French premiere, in concertante version, took place in summer 2009 as part of the "Musiques interdites" festival in Marseille. The CD released in 2011 by eda records (eda 35) is based on a live recording of a concertante performance on June 13, 2010 in the Lutosławski Studio of Polish Radio in Warsaw. The performances on August 17 and 18, 2014 at the Bregenz Festival were the Austrian premiere and at the same time the first staging of the work.

has never been as wide in the history of Western music as it was at the time of the opera's composition. In this way, the opera dissolves, in the form of a musical utopia, the many experiences of not belonging that weighed on Laks's artistic existence.

The melody, which the journalist intones as a hymn to the song's immortality, is a contrafacture. Laks borrows it from himself. It's his melody for the poem by Julian Tuwim *Prósba o piosenkę* (*Request for a Song*), one of the most important Polish lyric poet of the first half of the 20th century.

> **Request for a Song**[18]
> Seeing as I possess the word, oh Creator, your marvelous gift,
> Make my heart beat with the fury of the oceans,
> Make me simple and noble like the olden poets,
> Such that I can hit the powerful and the tyrants
>    with the gale of my blood.
>
> Do not inspire me with hymns, as hymns are not needed
> by those who in their gnawed down chests under dirty shirts
> carry hungry hearts, crying out for a piece of bread,
> running behind the band that is playing in the last parade
>    for the kings.
>
> Instead, endow the words of my fury
>    with the glint of sharp steel,
> With bravado and imagination,
>    with accurate and graceful rhyme,
> So that those that I hit are struck straight in the head
>    with the bullet of a six-shot song.

---

18. Translated by Howard Weirner for the complete recording of Laks' songs by the label eda records.

The depth of this work, so light on the surface, is revealed here at last. Tuwim, also of Jewish origin, was able to leave Poland after Hitler's invasion, and survived the war and extermination by going into exile in the United States. The rewriting of his request for a "six-strike song" as an apology for the melody which, in its immateriality, transcends all boundaries and achieves immortality, can be interpreted in several ways. As in a palimpsest, the hidden Tuwim text can be read as a smuggled message. Or it may be a comment by the composer, who recognizes that the powerful cannot be brought down with the weapons of poetry, but that poetry will outlast the powerful. That Laks has applied the "great animals"' trial of the swallow to his own situation, that he is in fact himself in this trial, is made clear by another self-citation within the opera. Just as the journalist is about to explain to the animals the true identity of the "swallow of the suburb," the dove interrupts him and reminds him of protocol: "Sir, you have the great honor of being able to attend a very rare ceremony. So there's only one thing left for you to do: not a word, not a gesture!" In the song, the middle part of which Laks quotes at this point, one of his melodies is heard again, accompanying a text by Tuwim. This is a correction—*Erratum* is the title of the poem—to be made to the book of life.[19] "A dark error has crept into my life/Hence the obscure passages and disorders of the text." It is not 40 lines, but 40 years earlier, that the lyric self asks the creator or fate to replace "despair" with "love." Surprising not only is the parallelism between Tuwim's text and the rupture in Laks's own life—in 1941, the year of his internment, he was exactly 40 years old—but above all its superimposition on the opera's "ceremony," which in fact resembles a legal proceeding. Both are about selection—and the survival of music.

---

19. *Erratum* appeared together with *Wszystko* (*All*) and three other songs written between 1936 and 1938 on poems by Tuwim in 1968 under the title *Pięć pieśni do wierszy Juliana Tuwima* (*Five songs on poems by Julian Tuwim*) with the Polish music publisher PWM.

Laks, stylistically close to neoclassicism in the broadest sense, ended his musical career in the late 1960s because he felt that there was no more room for him in a musical field dominated by serialism and post-serialism. Shocked by the 6-Day War and the new wave of anti-Semitism sweeping Poland, he ceased to believe in the meaning of artistic activity. His last substantial work is the charming *Divertimento for flute, violin, cello and piano* from 1966,[20] in the slow movement of which he inserts a melancholy melody from his opera. The tortoise sings at this point: "Alas, alas, violent death/is nowadays frequent." After meeting Władysław Szpilman at a guest concert of the Warsaw Quintet in Paris, he adapted his *3rd* String *Quartet* into a *Piano Quintet*, and published a *Suite concertante* for trombone and piano with the Polish music publisher PWM, two movements of which are identical to the *Three Concert Pieces* of 1933 mentioned above.

A 1974 reunion with Ludwik Żuk-Skarszewski, to whom Laks owed his survival in Auschwitz and whom he mistakenly believed had died in the camp, led him to set two of his poems to music. Laks, an incorruptible spirit and clear-sighted observer of world history, then definitively exchanged the composer's pencil for the polemicist's sharp pen. He translated Polish dissident literature into French and, from 1976 until his death in 1983, published a series of books in which he took a stand on the most diverse themes, from literature to the political events of the day. Old and new anti-Semitism remained a leitmotif of his writings.

Laks' fate is by no means singular. The destruction of Polish musical life between 1939 and 1945 and the systematic persecution

---

20. The work also exists in a version for violin, clarinet, bassoon and piano.

of Polish composers of Jewish origin in Europe[21] involved countless trajectories and inflicted indescribable damage on European cultural history. Many important composers were killed, and their work destroyed. We might mention Józef Koffler, the most important representative of the Second Viennese School in Poland, or Joachim Mendelson. Some survived the extermination, like Simon Laks, thanks to a series of miracles and the courageous help of compatriots, like Władysław Szpilman, Tadeusz Kassern and André Tchaikowsky. Some managed to escape in time, like Miezysław Weinberg, Roman Haubenstock-Ramati, Alexandre Tansman, Jerzy Fitelberg, Karol Rathaus, Ignace Strasfogel and Paul Kletzki. With the exception of Weinberg, who has been enjoying something of a renaissance in recent years—more as a Soviet composer than a Polish one—most of them remain unknown to today's audiences. Having fallen between the cracks due to their life in exile, they go completely unnoticed by a musical establishment entirely fixated on defined national identities.

But what is one to make of Simon Laks' trajectory, a composer who had to play in the immediate vicinity of the gas chambers? After Laks experienced this traumatizing contrast between a life "for" music and survival "through" music, he reserved music for himself after the war as a place of freedom. Humor and irony, which already characterized his musical language before the war, did not disappear from his vocabulary. His major work is an *opera buffa*. If Adorno thought it impossible to compose poetry after Auschwitz, how could an Auschwitz survivor compose a comic opera? The humor in Laks' music—at least in that composed after his liberation from Auschwitz—has a hidden component: it constitutes a means

---

21. The persecution affected not only composers of Jewish origin, but Poland's entire cultural and intellectual elite. See Elżbieta Markowska, Katarzyna Naliwajek-Mazurek: *Okupacyjne losy muzyków. Warszawa 1939-1945* (*The destiny of the musicians during the occupation*, Warsaw 1939-1945) published by Towarzystwo im. Witolda Lutosławskiego (Witold Lutosławski Society).

of distancing, a tightrope act above the abyss of horror. Shortly after 1960's *Petite suite légère*, whose *Polka* contains a good bit of *Ubu*, he set to music Antoni Słonimski's *Elegy for Jewish Villages*, one of the most poignant lyrical texts in the Polish language on the annihilation of Jewish life and culture in Poland.

The Polish contribution to the music of the 19$^{th}$ and 20$^{th}$ centuries is marked by exile to a far greater extent than those of other Eastern European countries. The creation and lives of composers like Laks invite us to take a closer look at a central aspect of European cultural history: transculturality and transnationality. All the composers mentioned above broke out of their national contexts and forged a style that was as individual as it was universal, in confrontation with the most diverse currents of the European avant-garde of their time. At a time of reflection on European identity, we find here the starting points for a new perspective on music history that could broaden the reductive gaze cast on national singularities and schools, and direct our eyes and ears to the many reciprocal influences, across borders, at the heart of 20th-century music, which is characterized more by what binds than by what separates. The "error," as it says in Tuwim's poem, which is inscribed in the lives of these composers, must not remain the criterion that defines their place in the history of 20th-century music.

# GLOSSARY

*"Arbeit macht frei":* "Work makes you free". Inscription above the entrance gate of the Auschwitz camp.

'*Berliner Luft'* : German song, 'Berlin Air'

Block: inmate barracks.

*Blockführer* : head of block

*Canada* (*Kanada*) nickname given by the prisoners to the area where the goods extorted from the deported Jews were stored and which symbolized a remote wealth.

Commando: group of prisoners in charge of various types of work and activities. There was for example a commando of carpenters, a commando in charge of the maintenance of the barracks, a disciplinary commando, a 'clearing commando' (see Canada) and a 'special' commando (see *Himmelskommando* and *Sonderkommando*).

*Crematorium*: usually refers to a place where corpses are burned. At Auschwitz-Birkenau, it also refers to the killing facilities, which included gas chambers crematoriums

'*Deutsche Eichen*' : German song, 'German Oaks'

*Effektenlager:* barracks where the prisoners' stolen belongings which were going to be sent to Germany, were stored (second step after *Canada*).

Gestapo: Secret State Police, one of whose offices in Poland was in Auschwitz I (Reich Territory).

*Hauptsturmführer:* military rank of the SS equivalent to captain.

'*Heimat deine Sterne*': German song, 'Fatherland, your stars'

*Himmelkomando:* literally "sky commando", a term in the camp slang that ironically referred to the *Sonderkommando* in charge of gassing the prisoners and burning their corpses.

*Kalifaktor:* domestic.

*Kapelle* : orchestra

*Kapellmeister*: orchestra conductor

*Kapo:* a prisoner (male or female) who was given the function of supervising the prisoners in the commandos and the power to perform services. They were often common law prisoners.

*Kommando*, see Commando

*Kraut*: boche

*Lager*: the camp

*Lagerältester:* general supervisor of the camp.

*Lagerarzt:* camp doctor

*Lagerführer:* SS camp commander

*Lagerkapelle:* camp orchestra

*Musikstube:* music room

*Muslim :* in the slang of the camp, designates a prisoner that exhaustion and hunger have made unable to react, prostrate, dying. The origin of the term is disputed. One hypothesis is an allusion to the prostration of the Muslim prayer, mocked by the Nazis.

*Notenschreiber:* copyist of scores

*Oberkapo:* principal Kapo

Organization, to organize, get organized: in the camp jargon, to get something by one means or another, bartering, trafficking, scavenging, stealing.

# GLOSSARY

*Prominent:* prisoner enjoying certain privileges because of his functions in the camp.

Ramp: arrival platform for the convoys of Jewish deportees on which the "selection" was carried out. Two ramps operated successively: the *Judenrampe*, located between the two camps, and then from May 1944, the ramp located inside the Birkenau compound between camps BI and BII.

*Rapportführer:* officer in charge of discipline.

*Reichsdeutscher:* German of the Reich.

*Revier:* pseudo-infirmary for prisoners. Selections were held there.

*Rottenführer:* military rank of the SS equivalent to lieutenant.

*Sonderkommando:* literally "special commando", crematorium commando (see also *Himmelkommando*). The members were periodically eliminated and replaced in order to maintain secrecy.

*SS:* abbreviation of *Schutzstaffel* ("Protection Squadrons"), Nazi paramilitary and police organization, created in 1925 to ensure Hitler's personal guard and directed by Himmler. From 1939, the SS were in charge of the internal security of the Reich and then of the occupied territories. They directed the administration of the camps and implemented the extermination of the Jews and Gypsies.

*Sturmmann:* military rank of the SS equivalent to lieutenant.

Triangles: Each prisoner wore, sewn on the left side of his jacket or dress, a cloth band with his number and a colored triangle (red on another yellow forming the Star of David for Jews, red for political prisoners, green for common law prisoners, brown for gypsies, pink for homosexuals, and purple for Jehovah's witnesses). A letter printed on the triangle indicated the nationality.

*Unterscharführer:* military rank of the SS equivalent to sergeant.

# GLOSSARY

*Volkssturm:* popular militia created in 1944 by the Nazis in the last months of the war.

*Wehrmacht:* German army.

*"Zu fünfe!":* an order, "Put yourself in groups of five!"

# FIRST READERS

Reese Wachob  USA
Marju Vroman  USA
Liam Nolan  ENGLAND
Heather Colley  ENGLAND
Alexandra Grunberg  ENGLAND
Hannah Schneck  AUSTRIA
Thomas Trezise  USA
Peter Miller  USA
Sarah Hammerschlag  USA
Adriana von Franqué  GERMANY
Marc Amfreville  FRANCE
Volker Hagedorn  GERMANY
Glenn Most  ITALY
Yaira Pinillos  USA
Frank Beninato  USA
Colleen Brackett  USA
Michelle Rosen  USA/FRANCE
Brendan Oregan  IRELAND
Brian Zielenski  TAIWAN
Sophie Simonelli  FRANCE
Karine Actis-Borgatti  FRANCE
Olivia Lewi  FRANCE
Heather Colley  UK
James Thatcher  UK
Alex Fang  CHINA
Makana Eyre  USA